Return to Center
— *Hocokan Unkupi* —

Return to Center
— *Hocokan Unkupi* —

Tokala Two Elk
as told to J. Dawn Jones

White River Press
Amherst, Massachusetts

Copyright 2024, Tokala Two Elk
All rights reserved.

Published by White River Press
Amherst, Massachusetts • whiteriverpress.com

ISBN: 978-1-935052-99-9

Book cover and interior designed by Lufkin Graphic Designs
Norwich, Vermont • www.LufkinGraphics.com

Cover and chapter illustrations by John Beheler
Photos from the author's collection

Library of Congress Cataloging-in-Publication Data

Names: Two Elk, Tokala, 1953- author. | Jones, J. Dawn, author. | Beheler, John, illustrator.
Title: Return to center : hocokan unkupi / Tokala Two Elk ; as told to J. Dawn Jones ; illustrated by John Beheler.
Description: Amherst, MA : White River Press, [2024]
Identifiers: LCCN 2023020757 | ISBN 9781935052999 (paperback)
Subjects: LCSH: Lakota philosophy. | Lakota Indians--Rites and ceremonies.
Classification: LCC E99.T34 T95 2023 | DDC 191.089/975244--dc23/eng/20230519
LC record available at https://lccn.loc.gov/2023020757

*This book is dedicated to my grandparents and great-grandparents,
Earth Nation Woman (Wounded Knee Survivor),
Nettie Buffalo Horn Chips, Robert Two Elk, and Hehaka Nunpa;*

to my parents, Phillip and Nellie Two Elk;

and to my family—

*my kids: Claude Miles Two Elk, Nellie Rae (Tuki) Two Elk,
Hehaka Nunpa Two Elk*

and

my adopted (**Hunka**) *children:*

Crystal Brave Eagle, Adian Zlotak;

and all those who I tied a feather or plume to;

and to all my adopted family globally,

and

Star Relatives (**Wicahpi Oyate**).

Mitakuye Oyasin
(ALL MY RELATIVES)

Le Miye Yelo

Tokala Hocokan Waokiya ob mani

Wopila Tanka Icicya Pelo
A Big Thank You

for sharing your knowledge and wisdom which has helped those of us who are reaching out:

Canupa Wakan – Tukasila – Grandfather – Wakan Tanka – Tatuwe Topa;
To all my past Tunkasilas/Grandfathers who are in the Spirit World.

To my Hunka Brother, Dr. A. C. Ross – Teacher

His Research – Spirit Author

Leksi Charlie Kills Enemy – Medicine Man – Pejuta Wicasa (Spirit World)

Mom and Dad (Spirit World)

Grandpa Sam Moves Camp – Medicine Man (Spirit World)

Leksi Frank Arrow Side – Medicine Man (Spirit World)

Tahansi Sam Moves Camp – Medicine Man

Leksi Rudy Runs Above – Medicine Man (Spirit World)

Brother Charlie Long Soldier – Life Saver

Dr. Martin Broken Leg – Teacher

Tahansi Gene Thin Elk

Tiblo Alex Lunderman Sr.

my sisters, Inez and Twellie Two Elk

my brother, Douglas Two Elk

my nephew, Joyle Two Elk

my daughter, Nellie Rae Two Elk

my son, Hehaka Nunpa

I would also like to say a big Wopila to those who helped get this book published including Jami Bartgis, J. J. Lind, Eric Noyes, Lynn Stegner, Amy and Doug Burns, Mary Bisbee-Beek, Abby Rush, Oak Lake Writers Society, and the Elders Wisdom Project of the Seventh Generation Fund for Indigenous Peoples.

Always remember to thank your enemies, and those who have hurt you, but pray for them, that they will someday open their eyes, ears, heart, Spirit. Those who have hurt you have also given you a teaching, one that you will never forget.

Try to shake their hand, in this world. It is okay if you do not. You have done your part, let it go, get on with your life.

Contents

Foreword i

Preface v

Timeline 1

Otokahe (In the Beginning) 7

Wakan Wicoicahe (Sacred Stages of Life) 14
    Teachings of **Wo, Wa, Wi, We** 18
    Universal Laws 20
    Sacredness of the Black Hills, a Sleeping Giant 30
    The Impact of Catholicism on WoLakota 34
    Dreams That Give Life 44

— PART 1 —

Wowakan Kicopi (The Calling)
    The Good and the Bad, the Yin and the Yang 50
    Sacred Energy 52
    The Medicine of Humor 60
    We Come from the Spirit World 62
    Circle of Life 66
    Calling the Spirit Back and Wiping of the Tears 68

— PART 2 —

Wowakan Cekiyapi (The Welcoming)
    Creating Balance for the Mind and the Spirit 78
    Puberty Rights 83

— PART 3 —

Wowakan Skan Skanpi (Healing/Living Energy/Action)
    Movement of Sacred Dirt 87
    Generosity 97
    Spiritual Trauma of Indoctrination 99
    Homeless 109
    Understanding the Third Gender 112
    Energy of Anger 114
    Memorial 122
    Teachings about Suicide 123
    Energy of Greed 126
    Historical Trauma Creates Our Current State 129
    Mixed Bloods 143
    Sacred Children 145
    The World's Shortest Prayer 152
    Through the Mouth You Live Sacred 155
    Making Relatives 162
    Receiving a Name 168
    Third Door and Medicine of Adulthood 170
    Power of the People 172
    Stages of Understanding WoLakota and
        How Freud Got It Wrong 176

— PART 4 —

Wowakan Glustanpi (Releasing/Letting Go)
    Look This Way, This Is Me 179
    Wakan Elderhood 187
    Giving Your Spirit, Mind, and Body Rest and Relaxation. 193
    Releasing the Monster 195

— THE HEALING —

Ina Maka Wiconi
    Spirit Thanksgiving 205

Appendix. 207

Tokala Two Elk, His Life in Photos 211

Foreword

I HAVE KNOWN TOKÁLA TWO ELK for most of our lives. We are nearly the same age, grew up on the same reservation, and have had contact at various times throughout our lifespans. I have even moved to Uŋčí Makȟá, Grandmother's Country, Canada, where he lived for a time. I know many of the people he refers to in this autobiography, as well as some of the community events he refers to. Of course, in our youthful days I knew him as Claude. He attended a school that my father administered, and so he was one of the "Hare School boys."

As a longtime instructor of First Nations Studies and an educator of Indigenous students, Tokála offers *Return to Center* as a classic example of how a Traditional Lakȟóta would explain himself. This is ***wicóuŋčağe***—a term that literally means a generation, but also can mean one's life story, or one's lineage. In typical Lakȟóta fashion, Tokála draws on many aspects of communication to relate his experiences. He uses a narrative format to explain law, education, theology, history, and ethnology; he uses reminiscence and poetry to explore his personal experiences and semantic nuance; he uses storytelling to explain sacred and mythical teachings and theology; and he explores his life and thoughts in a clear, comprehensive manner by relating connections and associations and not in a didactic lecture format.

This is Tokála's telling of his life experiences, the credentials that Lakȟóta people understand as his experiential diplomas.

This is also Tokála's waktóglaka—his recounting of his battle experiences. In an oral culture, a person explains his authority and authenticity by retelling his experiences; he does not rely on printed certificates and signed diplomas to give him authority. Lakota culture values experiential learning above all other ways of learning, except for direct revelations from the spirit world. A true Lakota recounts his experiences truthfully and leaves it to the listeners to understand his authority. He will not explain his authority, lest he devalue the ability of his listeners to understand what he has learned.

Like all human beings, Tokála was born with the spiritual skills to be strong and to survive. Traditional Lakota culture provides the experiences that educate a child's heart to survive the hardships of life: these experiences are the specific skills I call The Circle of Courage. In his childhood, Tokála had most of the experiences that create the spiritual strength a psychologist would call resiliency. As a Lakota, Tokála faced the racism, economic hardships, and complexities of life that others have faced. But when each of these negative experiences were deficits, Tokála's spirit found the resilient spirit that enabled him to get up again. This is not a small thing, especially when one considers the astonishing degree of intergenerational trauma that Lakota and other First Nations have experienced from outside factors. Tokála confronted all of those hardships and is here to tell his story. That is resiliency. Resiliency cannot guarantee that a person will not have problems, but it can promote survival and renewal when hardships are faced and overcome. This is Tokála's waktóglaka, his triumph over the hardships with which he's been challenged in his life. Throughout this book, you will see how his thinking and practices have given him the spiritual strength to be a survivor.

The Center is the strongest spiritual place in Lakota ceremony. This life story is Tokála's return to his spiritual strength. It demonstrates the aspects of resiliency of many Lakota people—through which perhaps you will see your own.

~ Dr. Martin Brokenleg
Victoria, BC   Canada

Preface

*R*ETURN TO CENTER began from a common desire to make the world a better place for our future generations. Tokala Two Elk and I found one another while working together on a community grant project in South Dakota. Having never met before, we immediately connected through our shared desire to heal from the effects of historical and intergenerational trauma, and through our mutual vision of strengthening our communities through kindness, love, and compassion. After 4 years of working with each other, consulting on project documents to support community healing, we had lots of experience writing on the topic and had pushed one another in our way of thinking to strengthen our awareness and understanding of trauma and the healing journey. As a psychologist, I quickly recognized how deeply Tokala understood trauma and was able to teach good lessons about healing using a sacred and gentle vibration that people of all ages could understand.

When the community grant ended, he asked me to help him write this book. To say it was an honor would be an understatement. I knew he had stories that the entire world needed to hear, so I agreed to commit to the endeavor. With support from a dear friend, Tokala came to visit me in Oklahoma, and we created the bulk of this work over ten intensive days, and through other sessions that occurred by phone and in various settings in South Dakota when we could find time to meet. Throughout those writing days we laughed, we cried, we shared the fellowship of my friends and family, we participated in our local ceremonies and gatherings, and we dreamt of a future where all living beings of all nations and all planets would live in harmony with one another. We dreamt of a time when we can truly be at peace and in harmony with Mother Earth, the Animal Nation, and our relatives of the stars.

Writing this book, which we originally titled *Return to Blueprint*, was a layered process that was directed by Tokala and organized by me. My role was to document, support the flow of the writing in English, and conduct necessary research to summarize in the book in order to educate the reader. Given that Tokala learned English as a second language, he wanted this support. His hope was for the book to be easily understood in English, so it could be read around the globe. Therefore, he agreed to edits that supported the reader, such as clarifying and using consistent tense that was not always present in natural speaking.

In the beginning, he wanted to develop a table of contents, but by the end we had something completely different than what we had conceptualized, so the table of contents was created last. This book is not written in a linear fashion, but in concentric circles that continually weave together stories about our connection to the universe. To create the narrative, Tokala spoke and I typed. I am a fast typist, and he is a slow talker, so it worked. After we had about 100 pages of narrative, we started what we called the *Flesh It Out Process*. This is where I read every single line in every single paragraph multiple times until it suited him. His limitation in eyesight required reading sections ten times or more so he could process it by hearing. His responses included "No, that's not right," after which he would proceed to correct the narrative.

Or he would say, "Yes, but you need to add more." Anything he changed or added was reread to him over and over until he threw his hands up in the air and yelled, "Whoo Hoo!" That's when I knew we got it right and could move on. During this time of the *Flesh It Out Process*, I would point out any inconsistencies or gaps in the narrative and make suggestions for transitions. He also allowed me to add on to some of the narrative when I had ideas that could take his message even further, so long as he agreed with it. If he did not agree with my input, it was not included. To complete the finished manuscript, it took approximately five years and three major revisions to make sure it was just as he wanted.

Tokala wanted to include Lakota words throughout the book in order to speak to Lakota people. He was steadfast to spell the letters as he was taught to spell them, which does not include various accent marks or special characters. Tokala believes that if a person can speak Lakota, they are going to know what he is saying and how to pronounce it.

While this book took a tremendous amount of time, it was my honor and blessing. I learned more about who I am and my own healing journey, and I am forever changed. One day in October, Tokala left Oklahoma. I went home and saw the kitchen chair next to the front door that he sat in each day to put on and take off his shoes. I can still see him there with his beaded Native Pride hat holding down thin gray hair strands wisping in many directions like frozen blades of grass on a sunny day, his eyes framed by valleys that I now know he earned through the depth of his life experiences and incredible wisdom. I picture how he says, "Who me?" when everyone is waiting on him to talk, like he is humbly asking your permission for you to learn from him. I felt his good energy still there, so I sat down in the chair to be near the good feeling he left. As soon as I sat down the tears began to roll down my cheeks and fall onto my lap. They were tears of releasing, just like Tokala taught me should happen as the 4th stage of the ceremony. The tears were those of love and joy I had for his gentle Spirit, his good teachings, and his infectious laugh. The writing of this book was, indeed, a ceremony. One I will never forget! Seeing this book through to publication is my Thanksgiving to Tokala for trusting and believing in me and for helping me be a better person by sharing his teachings. In a time when the world is in chaos, he brings the wisdom we need to save ourselves. He brings the wisdom we need to save the world.

~ *J. Dawn Jones*

NOTE: Unless otherwise noted, throughout the narrative, I occasionally add a touchstone that applies to our conversation to share the context in which these stories were being told. Those are my words, not Tokala's, and are shown in both brackets and italics to differentiate from his voice.

~ *J. Dawn Jones*

Timeline

of the Life of Tokala Two Elk as Best Remembered by Tokala

1953   Tokala was born in Pass Creek on the Pine Ridge Reservation.

1959   Tokala was forced to enroll in school in 1st grade. This was also when he first received a U.S. birth certificate.

1962   Tokala moved to Wanblee at 9 years old with his parents, and his dad began drinking alcohol heavily. Tokala switched schools a lot as his family was picking potatoes in Nebraska.

1966   Tokala's dad died of cancer in the spring, and his mom enrolled him in the Bishop Hare Board Home, Episcopal Boarding School, in South Dakota.

1971   Tokala moved to Ohio at 18 years old and worked for three months at a Boy Scout camp.

1972   Tokala graduated from Todd County High School in South Dakota.

1973   Tokala began classes at Dakota Wesleyan University in Mitchell, South Dakota.

1974   Tokala got married to his first wife.

1975   Tokala and his first wife had a son and moved to Manitoba, Canada.

1977   Tokala returned from Canada and started school at Sinte Gleska University in Rosebud, South Dakota. Feeling lost, he identifies that alcoholism began for him, even though his first drink was much earlier during church communion.

1979   Tokala stopped drinking to finish college.

1980   Tokala received a bachelor's degree in Human Services from Dakota Wesleyan University. He worked one month over the summer at Red Horse Lodge in Fort Thompson as a counselor, and in the fall he went to work in Eagle Butte School District as a Lakota language coordinator across all of the schools.

1981   Tokala took a position at Todd County High School as a teacher of Lakota studies.

1982   Tokala got accepted to graduate school and began his graduate program at the University of South Dakota (USD) in Vermillion.

1983   Tokala married his second wife and they returned to his home to care for his mother who was ill. Tokala did not have children with his second wife. He began drinking again.

1984   Tokala's mom died from a hemorrhage.

1985	September 12 is the exact date Tokala stopped drinking and never went back to it. He and his second wife divorced shortly after. He began a director of counseling position at the Intensive Residential Guidance in Crow Creek High School (a boarding school).
1986	Tokala went back to USD to finish the coursework for a master's program in Education Administration through independent study while living in Crow Creek. However, he was not allowed to graduate since he took too long to complete the program and passed the statute of limitations. In the fall he took a position at the Flandreau Indian School as a home living specialist and girls' dorm director.
1989	Tokala met the mother of his second and third child, and they lived together in a tent for about three months near the canyons west of St. Francis. Then they moved into a boarded-up house in Two Strike that he cleaned up with permission from the Housing Authority. He paid rent on this house, and he applied for a home ownership program. He began working for an outpatient treatment center in St. Francis.
1990	Tokala and his family moved into a house in Two Strike that he eventually paid off in 1997 through the home ownership program. He still lives there today. He started working at Sinte Gleska as director of a Robert Wood Johnson Foundation grant, Lakol Wicoun, Lakota methods for healing and sobriety.
1992	Tokala's first daughter was born, his second child.
1993	Tokla continued at Sinte Gleska as a coordinator for a National Science Foundation (NSF) grant to integrate Lakota and culture into science and math.

1994   Tokala's second son was born, his third child.

1995   Tokala becomes the director of the bilingual program at St. Francis Indian School.

1996   Tokala becomes the Aberdeen Area Tribal Chairmen's Health Board, director of Alcohol Related Developmental Disabilities. Received master's degree from Oglala Lakota Tribal College, Managers as Warriors Program.

1997   The mother of his second and third child left the home in Two Strike. Tokala took a job as a grant writer for the Sicangu Lakota (Rosebud) Nation for a month or two and then took a position as the director of another NSF grant at Oglala Lakota Tribal College.

1998–2002   Tokala worked as a consultant for Haskell Indian School in Lawrence, Kansas, on two grants focused on cultural services for youth and families. He also worked as a consultant for Wahpeton Indian School, Sisseton Wahpeton Oyate treaty land, consulting on Lakota language grants, later working as a social worker for White River Nursing Home with the Rosebud Tribe. Following that, he worked as a substance abuse director for Marty Indian School, Ihanktonwan Nakota Oyate treaty land. He also served as the fire keeper at the Healing Mother Earth Conference in Virginia Beach.

2002–2014   Tokala worked for Juvenile Detention Center (JDC) as a youth wellness counselor.

2015   Tokala worked for the Lower Brule community as the director of a Substance Abuse and Mental Health Services (SAMHSA) Circle of Care grant.

2016	Tokala was elected to the Sicangu Rosebud Treaty Council.
2018	Tokala retired at age 65 and continues consulting with schools and organizations.
2019	Tokala applied for his first U.S. passport that was initially denied because he needed to "prove" he was born in the United States. With help from Senator Thune's office the passport was approved, and Tokala took his first trip outside of the United States to Guatemala to support healing across borders.
2020	Tokala traveled to Colombia in February to continue mobilizing Indigenous international healing.
2023	Tokala serves as the Chair of the Sicangu Lakota Treaty Council and continues the work to unite and heal the Oceti Sakowin Oyate.

Otokahe
(In the Beginning)

*J*ESUS WAS BORN IN A BARN, and I was born in a chicken coop. When we come into the world, we are always taught that who we see are our relatives. I always say **Mitakuye Oyasin**, which for me means, "All our relatives, including the chickens."

We Lakota believe in an energy called **Wowahocoka** (spiritual/mental advice), which is both positive and negative. Energy comes from the sacred vibrations that we make. Our Lakota language is very nasal, and there is something about the bone where your glasses sit on the top of the nose that vibrates more with the nasal *ahhhhhhhhhn* sound. Our people are always singing our prayers using sacred vibrations. When you sing a nasal *ahhhhhhhhn*, your nose bone vibrates. There is something about that bone vibrating that makes that third eye wake up. Other people's religions and beliefs call that third eye one of the Chakras. That nasal sound is a sacred vibration that wakes up your Chakra. The whole body becomes one big megaphone when you send a nasal *ahhhhhhhhn* into the world. It sends a message to the universe that is galactic. That message can be positive or negative. For example, when a woman is pregnant with a being that is closest to the Spirit World, she cannot think negative thoughts because her thoughts are so powerful they can be heard all over the universe, and she will impact the stars and the incoming Spirit.

So, I started making connections between other cultures and our Lakota culture. I started observing how many Asian cultures hit those big bells that made the sound, *GONG*, which is also like the sacred vibration made by the monks who chant, *ahhhhhhhhhhh*, with a long nasal sound to open up their third eye and connect with the universe. It is the same with our drum and the Lakota songs we sing.

Your body is a communication tool for the Spirit World. When your body speaks, the Spirits listen. Your atonement goes with your prayer. During my lifetime I observed elders using their body, mind, and Spirit to numb pain by chanting **Ceyanka** (moaning or groaning sound, expressing the pain for spiritual help). Crying is also a way your body communicates with the Spirit World. There is something about the act of crying. When you go on the mountain to fast or pray, you are communicating to God. When you really mean it, the tears come, and you do a releasing. That is why there are 4 parts to every ceremony.

There is the calling of your helpers or God's energy to open up your doors. This is like opening up your third eye, other Chakras, or the energy life flow called *Qi (Ch`i)* in Chinese, which the Lakotas call **Wo**.

Then there is the welcoming of your helpers. We all have one, two, or more helpers or guardians. Some people see them as angels. We Lakota don't see them as angels. We see them as bears, eagles, or other Spirit relatives of the winged, two-legged and 4-legged kingdoms.

The third part is healing, action, or movement. **Takuwakan Skan Skan** means something holy that has movement. I believe that all Indigenous people have the same examples of the connection to God and how to live with it. The Tribes from the East Coast, when the encroachment of the Europeans came, eliminated that process of connection that previously was intact within those Tribes.

The 4th part of the ceremony is thanking your helpers for coming and sending them home to the Spirit World.

But the ceremony doesn't stop there. You continue on. Your helpers just brought you energy and you can use it. They just made you stronger. It's ongoing. That's why we believe in the Circle. We don't see it in a linear way. Once the ceremony is over, it begins again.

The energy of God is in everything and is always moving, including Mother Earth that keeps spinning. Nothing stands still! Billions and billions of years of lands detached, lands attached, lands going underwater, lands coming up from water.

Many may not know this, but the Bible follows what we believe as Lakota people, and we are coming into the 4th cleansing.

The 4th Cleansing of the Christian belief is that the world will come to an end and begin again:

> *Revelation 21:1 ". . . And I saw a new heaven and a new earth: for the first heaven and the first earth were passed away."*

The prophecy of the buffalo consists of 4 legs (eras): the first leg is of a "healthy buffalo" when our people lived in prosperity; the second to the third legs lead up to the 4th leg, the exposure to the Europeans when we lost our way of survival. The 4th leg is when the buffalo was gaunt and hairless, and this one leg is the symbol of the women becoming leaders and not only Lakota women, but women universally. After the 4th leg there will be an era of peace. So the buffalo will return as a healthy animal again.

Life through the pipe came from one woman, **Pte San Win** (White Buffalo Calf Woman), and was given as a gift to two men. There is a reason for this. The woman brings the energy of love and love is life. I especially want men to know that the impact of colonization on Indigenous men was the perpetuation of violence, both internal (such as shame, guilt, substance abuse, etc.) and external (such as domestic violence and other abuses of the body, mind, heart, and Spirit of women). I want men to know that this is the disease from which men must be cured so that we can support the return of our women leaders to balance our lives and, therefore, the healing of Mother Earth. When women become leaders again, we will restore balance and harmony, the buffalo will recover again, and the entire Animal Nation will return to a time of peace and prosperity.

Today the buffalo stands on one leg as predicted from the Lakota prophecy. All living things are sick: water, land, animals, plants, and air. One of the impacts of colonization is that our women lost their power and are dominated by the dominant society. Because women are the creators of life, their role in leadership is necessary to restore the health and well-being of the planet, since they understand the protection of life more than any other gender. That's why we did the horse ride for 4 years to pray for our women. It ended in May 2018. It started in 2014 with the Sacred Horse Society to pray for the woman's Spirit to come back to the circle, to the **Hocoka**. I don't think we put a dent in repairing the damage that has been done to our women because of the trauma they have endured for so long at the hands of men who do not understand and practice universal law. That is the sickness that I see.

When I hear the young boy sing:

Send a voice for me, pray/cry for me, whatever you pray for will come true.

> *Ho Ye Makiyayo, Ce Makiyayo* (sing 3 times)
> *Taku Ihe Hekun Iye Ce Tuktelo* (*ye* instead of *lo* for feminine)
> *Ho Ye Makiyayo, Yanipi Ktelo* (*ye* instead of *lo* for feminine)

When you cry you are praying. When the priest or preacher says, "Let us pray" for Lakota that means, "Let us cry."

I always sing that song to the people. It has a meaning to it and that same Spirit is singing that same song in the invisible world. Both children and families are crying from what has been done to us. That we are so far away from the universal law that we feel helpless. And the life of substance use is growing because of this unresolved trauma. That's the reality we live in today.

One day in 2017, I saw on national television a huge Women's March that was going on in Washington, D.C. and in other cities across the United States. Women were there to bring their loving energy together, toward equality and the future of the people, of all people. This makes me feel good, that that nurturing energy is going to return to heal the sickness. In our own Tribal elections, we are seeing more women running for Tribal Council seats, and now two Indigenous women have been elected to the U.S. Congress. The women's movement is now global. This is what we were praying for within the Sacred Horse Society. The eagle staff that we carried during the ride had an image of a woman with no face. Underneath that image are 300+ eagle plumes representing the children who died during their forced relocation to Fort Snelling, Fort Thompson, and Santee. Before the ride we recognized that the traumas that happened to our people came from the first fire on the East Coast that was disrupted by Europeans.

The men need to acknowledge in this energy of movement and change that we must help the women so we may survive. Now we are in a time of energy that has been prophesied, and it is coming true. It is time for us to blend and unite with all two-leggeds to get back in balance and harmony with the world. I believe this is a calling from Mother Earth for all nations to address her pain.

When I was a kid, my grandpa said that the greedy ones should find gold on another planet so they can all get on rockets and space vehicles and leave our planet, so we may heal and recover from what they have done, to restore our balance and harmony. But the greedy ones are like termites. They will eat the bark off of live trees, leaving them unstable and vulnerable to disease and death, before they move on to another tree. How do we educate the termite to not eat all the trees? How do we heal them from the sickness that they carry?

For us to help each other, we need to educate on the 7th direction, which is ourselves. We need to heal and recover from the trauma, grief, and loss to make ourselves stronger and help each other to survive. One person cannot do it alone because it's global. It will take all of us united. Everything that has spiritual energy is medicine for us to live.

To fulfill the Lakota prophecy, our women must return to leadership and have power among us again (as it was in the past before the colonizer came) for gender balance to be restored, which also includes the gender or the people of two Spirits, having masculine and feminine energies. The entire world also needs this gender balance for the children to live. The genders of today need to create unity and work together to create a better life for our future generations. When gender balance is restored, the balance between all living beings will also be restored and the healing of Mother Earth will occur. Then the whole prophecy starts over again.

The Hopi have similar prophesies about a 4th cleansing, as do many other Indigenous peoples and religious groups.

In the **Hocoka** (Circle of Life) two energies exist, positive and negative. In the middle of the **Hocoka** there is a red road, which is the balance of our life, the balance of the positive and the negative. The Red road goes north and south, which represents balance and harmony. The Black road runs east and west, which represents life and death. When you choose to walk the red road, it is a little bit of both as it goes right down the center.

My relatives, I want to speak about the beginnings, so we may *return to our Blueprint*, which is in our blood, our genetic DNA.

When we return to our Blueprint, we are returning to our Center. What I absorbed growing up while listening to my elders I am going to share with you, so our young and old who are looking for understanding can carry this towards the future with good harmony and walk on Mother Earth.

With the knowledge of reawakening, coming into full understanding that day in Bear Butte, I learned that what was taught to me during my early years of life was so precious and life giving; full of energy, of life, and how to live a good one. It was inside me. What was taught to me was survival. The stories I tell in this book are what I can share with our Lakota people, other Tribal people, and all people of the world, to hang onto those old teachings, to hang onto Mother Earth and all of our relations. The stories told in this book are my understanding and experiences, but many details have been changed to protect people's privacy. The use of relative terms like "cousin" or "aunt" are used so as to not identify anyone directly. I use Lakota words as I was taught. Other people may have their own experiences and teachings of history or practices that are similar or different from mine. This is good, as it brings us a more complete picture of the **Hocoka** (Circle of Life).

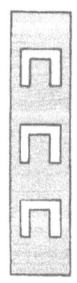

Wakan Wicoicahe
(SACRED STAGES OF LIFE)

An Introduction to the 4 Parts of Ceremony

*L*IFE IS A CEREMONY. All ceremonies involve 4 parts: Calling, Welcoming, Healing, and Releasing. About 160 years ago, and in the time before, the Spirit inside humans prayed for a good Spirit to come into their family. This calling is the first **Wakan**, (holy/sacred) connection that is made in the 4-part ceremonial process for a Spirit to manifest as a human being. It is something we do every day as a two-legged Spirit, but we are not aware of this. When a woman becomes pregnant, we are calling a Spirit into this world.

The second part is welcoming, which occurs when the womb creates life. There are good vibrations and nurturing from a mother's energy, which occurs when a Spirit is being welcomed to come to earth. Her health and wellness—physically, mentally, and spiritually—are connected to this welcoming part of the ceremony. For 9 months it is very critical for a mother to be in balance and good harmony so that the welcoming of the Spirit will occur. The sacred connection between father and mother, the balance and harmony in good vibration with the unborn Spirit, and the energy of the mothers during the 9 months of pregnancy creates a bonding energy and the foundational grounding for the Spirit coming into this world. During this time of pregnancy if there is any negative energy in the mother's **Hocokan** (Circle of Life—the "n" is added to demonstrate a personal circle rather than a global one which is spelled **Hocoka**), the Spirit inside will feel this and the Spirit may leave. A Spirit can come and go during the time of pregnancy, up until the hole in the baby's head hardens, as the elders have said.

Every one of our cultures (or races) had a hoop or **Hocoka** that was broken. Once this circle was broken, anger, hatred, resentment, and negative energy started to control us. If anger controls us, then we look for revenge, which leads us to produce negative vibrations, which we pass on to whoever is in our **Hocoka,** including our children, spouses, relatives, and friends. Those negative vibrations can impact the body, mind, and soul (or Spirit) of those around us. The 7th direction, which is within all of us, has the ability to pick up on those negative vibrations. During this time we have a choice. We can remain with the negative, or we can leave. Sometimes during the welcoming stage, when the Spirit is unhappy with the negative vibrations it is receiving and also when there is no spiritual grounding or anchoring from the mother or the father, the Spirit may leave this earth. A single thought of not wanting the baby can cause the Spirit to leave. I believe this is crib death or SIDS (sudden infant death syndrome), which may upset some people. Doctors are still trying to find a scientific answer, when it is really an unhappy and lonely Spirit. This may be difficult for many to grasp.

During the welcoming stage, both mom and dad must produce good vibrations of **Wowahwala** (unconditional love) and nurturing—songs, prayers, light smudging of cedar, sage, or sweetgrass—to clear the **Hocokan** of negative energy so that good energy of balance and harmony can be there to welcome that baby. Proud mothers and fathers prepare for the birthing by being in balance and harmony physically, mentally, and spiritually.

Currently, I recommend fathers to be involved in the birthing, welcoming of this Spirit into their family. I will tell you more about that later. In the past, midwives who were mothers, older aunts, or grandmothers welcomed the Spirit and made a commitment for the family to raise the Spirit in a positive way—a nurturing environment—all before the umbilical cord was cut.

The welcoming and bonding of parents and the new Spirit (baby) into the family is very important. The heartbeat of a mother during those 9 months is the nurturing sound of vibration of the womb, and is the heartbeat of the Spirit. One of our sacred Lakota rites is the **Wo Inipi** (through the mouth you live), which is better known as the *Sweat Lodge*. **Wo Inipi** symbolizes the womb of our mothers. Once the door is closed, there is no light in the **Wo Inipi** except the glow of the Grandfather Stones. If we stay there for the duration of the **Wo Inipi** Ceremony, our Spirit will connect with **Tunkasila** (Creator, Grandfather), the **4 sacred directions,** and **Tatuwe Topa,** (higher power). Our Spirit will remember the womb and unconditional love. The drum is the heartbeat in the **Wo Inipi**. When we are in the **Wo Inipi**, our Spirit will remember that heartbeat and will reconnect with **Tunkasila** (Creator).

The welcoming of the child will last up to the end of the **Wakan yeja** (sacred two-legged) stage, and the ceremony of the Puberty Rite. For girls, this is when they reach their first menstrual cycle called **Isnatipi** (living independently), and for boys, it is when their voice starts to change, and their rite is called *wohumbleceya* (crying for a vision).

During the welcoming, good positive energy must be practiced for this Spirit to grow up to be a **Waste** (good) adult.

The third and next aspect of the ceremony is healing, which is the time when purpose, or reason for being here, must be activated. There is a Blueprint for every one of us to become what we are supposed to become, a Spirit with positive energy that shares our sacred gifts with the world. We must heal when we are sick in order for us to be healthy leaders and human beings.

The 4th aspect is releasing, the letting go of what is hurting you. That is when thanksgiving occurs. Lakota practice thanksgiving with many expensive gifts in honor of our loved ones, accomplishments, or good health. We give with pride in our family names, in name giving ceremonies and memorials, among others that call for thanksgiving.

Gifts and money are usually saved up all year for these ceremonies. Star blankets, Pendleton blankets, shawls, materials, beadwork, and artwork are given away freely to the community.

Some of the poorest families put on the more lavish thanksgiving ceremonies, practicing **WoLakota-Wocanteognake** (generosity), because of their ability to save and help each other. Today, because of unemployment, family break-ups, alcoholism, drugs, gambling, too many early deaths, graduations, honorings, memorials, and plain survival, people cannot save (prepare), so the ceremony cannot be completed. In order for us to be successful, the family will have to work together to help each other and make these ceremonies a success.

These 4 parts of ceremony are a cycle, a pattern or process that has been lived for generations, and we don't even realize we are in it.

Teachings of
Wo, Wa, Wi, We

[During one of our writing sessions in the Ho-Jo (Howard Johnson) in Chamberlain, South Dakota, we sat in the "business meeting room," which was just a long collapsible table and a few folding chairs facing a window overlooking the indoor pool. We drank lots of free coffee, which I really needed after I had been working all day at a nearby Tribe. Tokala spoke for two hours about "Wo, Wa, Wi, We" before we boiled it down to this narrative . . .]

*L*AKOTA WORDS ARE ***Wo**, **Wa**, **Wi**,* and ***We*** (pronounced Weh).

Wo words are spiritual from the invisible (Spirit) world. It's like God's energy or God's love. Wo words are universal law. *If the Spirit is wounded, it is deeper than a mental wound and takes longer to heal.*

Wa words are mental and are used by the Animal Nation daily as we live on Mother Earth. When words have ***Wowa*** they are both spiritual and mental. They include both words because that will affect both our spiritual and mental balance. *If the mind is wounded, it is deeper than a physical wound and takes longer to heal.*

Wi is anything to do with and under the sun as a translation, and represents the physical. We always referred to the sun as father, ***Ate Wi*** (Father Sun). Father Sun gave the energy or vibration of love to Mother Earth so that all living energies could grow. Thought to be the world's smartest man, Einstein said that the sun sends vibrations, and we Lakota know it is vibrations of love from Father Sun to Mother Earth. There is even a website we can go to and hear it: youtube.com/watch?v=CRu_hG3X3bI.

Energy can be both positive and negative. The Lakota respect the negative as much as the positive.

We (pronounced Weh) . . .

We means blood. In the past, and in respecting the blood, universal law says we do not mix our blood with our relatives or we will create an imbalance. Today, this is not always respected. "No one is related after six o'clock," an elder at one community said.

Woope Otokahe
(The Laws of Blue Energy to Live)

Universal Laws

For Lakota, you must understand, respect, and live the universal laws, as they keep balance and harmony in the universe. These universal laws are how we all got along. Originally, they were considered spiritual laws but later were referred to in common man language as "values." Generosity, bravery, fortitude, and wisdom are the main universal laws but there are others. Wisdom is always the last. The reason our elders taught this is because we must use our wisdom to maximize the others in our lifetime. We must have the first values before we can have wisdom.

There are three gifts that I was given in this life. The first gift was the out-of-body experience that allowed me to space travel. I'll talk more about that later. The second gift surfaced in the 1980s during a time when I was sober and we were heading to Menominee, Wisconsin, to a pow-wow, and I had a sense that something was happening to me. As we got closer to Menominee, I started hearing voices, and as we got closer to the pow-wow, the voices would come and go. I realized that what I was hearing were the thoughts of the young people walking down the road. I heard these young people thinking to themselves. I realized it wasn't in my head; I could hear their thoughts. As we got closer to them in the car, their thoughts got louder, and when we drove away from them their thoughts got quieter, smaller.

We drove over these hills into an Amphitheatre. When we arrived at the pow-wow, I heard a voice that sounded like Darth Vadar—very deep and masculine. It was coming from behind me. When I turned around it was a grandma standing there. She looked like a real grouchy grandma. That Darth Vadar voice I heard had come from her. Her mouth wasn't moving, but I heard her mind, or her Spirit, and it sounded demonic. I felt chills. Then I heard two little young boys with whiny voices. They sounded like 4- or 5-year-olds who were trying to get their way. I heard two of them. But when I turned to face the voices, they were coming from two grown men. Again, their mouths were not moving, but I heard their minds or Spirits and they sounded like kids wanting attention. That time when I was hearing people's thoughts or intentions it lasted from six o'clock in the evening until three o'clock the next morning. I even heard animal voices, not actual voices, but animals communicating off in the distance. It was like standing in a lake and feeling electricity after lightning strikes. It was immediate! I heard black bears running in the woods and a mother bear calling for her cub to come back.

Anyway, I thought I was going crazy and so it felt like I was in a giant web. I was right in the center of this web. I was really uncomfortable, and my mind wanted to get away from hearing those thoughts. I pulled away as fast as I could, but it was hard to get out of the web. I wasn't physically doing it, I was *spiritually* doing it. Even today, if I focus on someone for a while, I can start hearing their thoughts. In the old days a parent would take this child with gifts to a Medicine Man to help them bond with it in a good way.

The third gift that surfaced is that sometimes, if I look at someone for a long time, I can tell when they are going to die and how. I didn't like that in the past. It was scary for me. Again,

I didn't know who to talk to about that. At one point, I thought I got over it. I thought I got over it years ago. But as years go by, it's still in me. Now, I catch myself. Sometimes if I look at someone too long, it happens again. I quickly look away because I don't want to know those things. If I look away from them, I can't see those things anymore. Once I got older, to this point now, I began to realize that life and death are just the experiences we are having here, because we have a spiritual life that is longer than the life we have here on Mother Earth. It's a spiritual life that we all go back to.

There are three **Owanka** that I respect. **Owanka** is a Lakota altar that is like a key to unlock the door to communicate with the Creator. I finally spoke to my cousin, who has one of those altars, about what was going on with me. He told me I should have gone to a spiritual helper, a Medicine Man who would help me nurture that gift so I could control it.

In 1995, somebody rang the doorbell at the house we were living in. I went to see who was at the door and it was my cousin, the one who has an altar. He had a **Wopahta** (sacred or spiritual bundle). I invited him in, and he put the **Wopahta** on the table. I gave him some coffee and sat down with him. He told me a Medicine Man that used to be alive is now dead and wished for someone to carry on his altar, his bundle. So, he brought it that day to me because the family could not find a member of his family who would be able to carry on this good work. My daughter and son were both in my life at that time, they were both gifts from the Creator, and were my priorities. I have a lot of respect for some of the knowledge, the wisdom that was shared with me about being a Medicine Man and all the things a person has to go through. For me, I respected that. Anyway, he brought the bundle to me and asked me to continue on with this man's bundle. I said, I don't think I can. I have a son and a daughter now. The way the people are today, they use medicine without protocol.

I also told my cousin about what happened to my sister's family and how powerful the altar of the Medicine Man—whose bundle was on the table—was. It started when my sister lived in Los Angeles. She returned home to the Pine Ridge Reservation by bus with her two grandchildren, but she left her two adult sons living there. My sister's oldest son called her after she had returned home. He shared his concern that a woman in Los Angeles was controlling her second son. The oldest son reported that this woman was leading him down the road of drugs (meth), so my sister wanted her son back. The son couldn't leave the woman because he was addicted, and she was his supplier. At one point, the son wanted to come home. While her sons were still in Los Angeles, my sister went to this Medicine Man who helped her addicted son break away through ceremony. This gave him the strength to run away from the woman. I had given my sister an old van that I had repaired to help her get to Los Angeles in the first place, and she had left it there for her sons to use; when he ran away from the woman who was controlling him, the van was in need of some real repair again. This woman had the keys, so he had to short wire the van to get it started, and the radiator was leaking. It was the month of January when he drove the baloney skin tires through the mountains to Pine Ridge. The Spirits really helped him because that van barely made it back.

When he finally showed up at my house, he was really boney and had lost a lot of weight. We had a **Wopila** (Thanksgiving) for the closure of the ceremony my sister started for him. At the same time, she rescheduled the doctoring for him because of his nutrition. He had lost his vitamins and minerals, the nutrients in his body, and he was hearing voices. They had 4 nights of ceremony for him, and I was there. I saw how powerful it was. He got better.

This is an example of when ceremony closure occurred, and it worked out good. However, other people who did not complete the ceremony or follow this Medicine Man's instructions, brought harm to his family. The Medicine Man's wife passed on because of this, and he was heartbroken. That's when this Medicine Man said he was going to put his altar up because nobody was listening to him anymore and disrespecting his help. That was just one of many examples where people were not completing the Thanksgiving. I wanted to take care of my children, and I didn't want anything to happen to them, so I didn't go that route to take the altar. That's what I told my cousin.

There are things I have done and people I have seen that I don't want to talk about. Mainly, it is because of what I saw in my uncles and my grandpas who were Medicine Men. There were so many people wanting redemption, but they didn't follow instructions, and there were consequences to the Medicine Men when the people they were trying to help didn't obey. There are so many sick people out there, and they would come in cars, bumper to bumper, all wanting to go to ceremony, to sweat, to get saved or healed or something.

There are Medicine Men who have power and they can help you, but it's like a gatekeeper to the ***Tiopa*** (door or doorway). If they help you with their power, you may not always learn. So, you are still missing parts, and you need to get those missing parts yourself. [*Tokala stares up and to the left as he thinks for a long time about how to say something. Then he closes his eyes for a while longer. When he finally has an idea of what he wants to say, he begins with "um"*].

Medicine Men can't break universal laws without serious consequences for them and their families. For example, they can't make a person fall in love and can't bring someone back to life. If they do, they or their family might suffer.

A true Medicine Man can see the energy you have. You may have some partial understanding of your Blueprint, so the Medicine Man will give you just enough information so you will be able to learn what ***Tunkasila*** is trying to teach you, and then motivate you to continue on with your holistic journey of life. The Medicine Man controls the level of information for the level that you are. You may think you are ready, but you may not be.

People can go through thirty years of sobriety, but just because they don't drink doesn't mean they are healthy. If they still haven't done the holistic work for holistic health, they are not healthy. The Medicine Man will say the appropriate words to make someone feel okay, and then let you go through the experience you need to go through in life. You have to suffer a little bit more because you haven't learned something that you need to learn. There is physical suffering, mental suffering, and spiritual suffering (***Wokakija***). Suffering can be negative and positive. That's why we do ceremony. For men it is Vision Quest, Sundance, and Sweat Lodge. For women, they were already gifted with sacred energy to help them with procreating life, the monthly, and the 9-month ceremony.

I can't break universal law. I also can't help you when you are not ready because you won't understand this medicine. You may want a shortcut. A lot of people today want shortcuts. Instant gratification without suffering. That's what many people are looking for. They're like children still looking for their mom and dad. It's like their Spirit is saying, "When are you going to come home?" Sometimes Medicine Men get individuals in their ceremony, and they will say what the person wants to hear. Inside himself the Medicine Man is saying, "I can't help you for 9 months until you come back and you are ready to learn." They teach you how to swim and they take you out in the ocean and drop you off and say, swim back.

When you go to a Medicine Man, you should offer them tobacco and ask for advice or wisdom. When you offer tobacco and a Medicine Man takes it, it is ***Opagin*** (a spiritual contract). If he doesn't take it, then he is not going to help you. A good Medicine Man has a known altar that is respected; good things come from the altar through ceremony. Through ceremony we work on the things we need to heal.

When we get better, we come back to that spiritual leader to do the closure, the ***Woplia***, the Thanksgiving ceremony. Many of our people don't have that respect to do that anymore. They take their healing and run. That will cause bad things to happen. You must follow protocol when you are healed or when your prayers are answered. You must follow the protocol of Thanksgiving. That is the 4th part of ceremony. A major part of the releasing is Thanksgiving.

As one example, a woman was having a ceremony for her husband who had cancer. When she took him back for his usual monthly checkup, they learned that his cancer had gone into remission. Afterwards, the family came back and said they should go into a sweat, and the medicine person told the wife she had to do 4 Thanksgivings at every new moon at night. She was to come to the medicine person's house and bring the food, certain amounts of colors of tobacco ties, and they had to do a ***Wopila*** ceremony. Each quarter, at each new moon, she would need to do these things. She came and did it the first time as she was told. She came the second time. And then she got sidetracked and believed everything was completed, because her husband was better. She never came back. Her lack of completion affected the family of the Medicine Man. He had to carry some of the burden for the lack of completion of the ***Wopila*** ceremony. Some of the elders say if we stop it when it's not completed, the Medicine Man would lose his family members, which happened.

This is the whole reason why I chose not to take another man's altar at that time, for fear of the people he helped who did not follow his instructions for completion of ceremonies. I was afraid of retribution for being a Medicine Man. This, along with the love I had for my children. At that time, I told him I wouldn't take on that altar until my children were older. Today, we have many thankless people that cause the elimination of our good medicine. Our people are the ones who are killing our good Medicine Men, because they do not have that sense of respect and they do not follow instructions. By not following instructions, the Medicine Men deal with the aftermath, which can lead to lives being taken from a Medicine Man's family. That's how serious it is. I was afraid of that!

I see some of the dedicated ones that get educated in schools come back. Some can pick up these universal laws, and some can't. Those who can't, separate themselves from being part of the whole. They separate themselves from being part of the Nation.

In the *Document of Discovery: Unmaking the Domination Code*, Birgil Kills Straight teaches about 7 universal laws:

> ***Wacanteognaka***: To carry the welfare of the people in your heart (generosity).
>
> ***Wowaunsila***: To have pity and compassion for all living things.
>
> ***Waoyuhuni***: To have respect and honor everything that moves.
>
> ***Wowacintaka***: To have a great mind, to have fortitude, spiritual patience, to not give up.
>
> ***Wowahwala***: To be humble at all times.
>
> ***Woohitika***: To be guided by your own principles to discipline yourself so you can be brave/courageous.
>
> ***Woksape***: Wisdom or understanding once we learn the first six laws.

There are many other universal laws, but here I will share five more including:

> ***Wotakuye***: Spiritual awareness of all my relations (family), a universal law of relationships.
>
> ***Wowahokunkiya***: Spiritual advice for survival that comes from grandparents/elders.

Woayapi: Energy rubs off on children, good or bad. This is an invisible energy that is passed on and taken in.

Wokipajin: This translates to the English word, *jealousy*. When you don't have something good to say about your relatives' achievements or success, you may not have the same examples of achievement in yourself or family (**Hoka**). A person who has **Wokipajin** must get their life back in order or it will get worse, like an infection, and it will take away your generosity and the generosity of your offspring.

Wakunza: You must be careful what you think, speak, and act (behave) as you will bring that type of energy to yourself and those around you.

Woaigluhpa: This translates to whatever you do falls back on you. What energy you put out will come back to you (karma).

One of my uncles, whose altar I respect, has cars parked a half a mile from his house all the way to the highway practically every night from people asking for help. Every night they have a ceremony and people come wanting his help. That's basically his full-time job. So, anyway, it's still on hold for my decision to take his altar and be a Medicine Man. Once you take the altar you are a Medicine Man. I haven't told many people about these things I'm sharing with all of you. I just wanted you to know that is the respect I have for my Spirit. In English it is called your aura, your energy, your **Wo** in **Lakota** (**Wolakota**). My uncles had that power, and those living still do. They are really humble about it. They don't holler or shout at anybody. They don't show a lot of anger. They are very humble people, so I try to keep my balance by practicing what we were talking about earlier, respecting our energies.

Those Medicine Men/Women, who have given their all, sacrificing their loved ones, family, to help someone else's health and welfare should be recognized for their endeavors. Always tell these people ***Wopila***, thank you.

Woyukini
(Reawakening a Spiritual Energy)

Sacredness of the Black Hills, a Sleeping Giant

[The information presented in this chapter was shared in the most unlikely place, high in the mountains in San Rafael, Colombia, where Tokala and I participated in an international Indigenous exchange with Tribal healers and leaders from Central and South America. He shared with me that as we were climbing the mountain, he had some fear for his life, so he said a prayer and then let it go. Later, during this trip, he repeated many of the following teachings both in the mountains and in a large lecture hall with more than 100 young people and professors studying in the Pedagogy of Mother Earth program at the University of Medellín. When Tokala spoke about the Thunder and Lightning Nation, the thunder started rolling outside even though the sky was clear and there was no rain. After a few gasps and murmurs in the crowd, we sat in silence and listened for a moment as the Thunder Beings welcomed us and then retreated as quickly as they came. The look of shock on the participants' faces was priceless. I was a little surprised too . . .]

THE BLACK HILLS IS A SACRED BURIAL PLACE for the ***Oceti Sakowin Oyate***, which include 7 Council Fires of the Lakota, Dakota, and Nakota peoples. Before the Europeans came, we were one people united with one voice. Today we have been divided into different Tribes and different territories, but the 7 Council Fires still exist and will be united once again.

The Black Hills is a place of healing where our people bury our relatives when they pass on to the Spirit World. In the past this was done in the traditional way, and today people spread ashes there. During the winter months, the Black Hills provided sustenance for our people to live as we herded buffalo into that area for food. The Black Hills is where we still practice our ceremonies and spiritual way of life. The Black Hills is like our church.

The sacredness of the Black Hills represents all the colors of earth to connect us to the 4 cardinal directions and also to the other 3 directions that few people understand.

The 4 cardinal directions are:

First direction is west (black), the Thunder and Lightning Nation (***Wakinyan Oyate***). The Thunder and Lightning Nation is respected as the energy of grandfather, God, and symbolizes new life in the springtime and follows the spring ***Cansasa Ipusiye*** (Equinox).

Second direction is north (red), the Buffalo Nation (***Tatanka Oyate***). The Buffalo Nation is strength, endurance, fortitude, and good health.

Third direction is east (yellow), the Elk Nation (***Hehaka Oyate***). The Elk Nation represents the energy of love and is also the new birth or new energy.

4th direction is south (white), the Animal Nation (***Wamaka Skan***) or Moving Dirt Nation (***Wamakaskan Oyate***). The Animal Nation represents all living energy and life force, symbolizing 4-legged, two-legged, winged ones, those who live in the water, and under the ground. Animal Nation, that's us.

When the ancestors used the term **Wamakaskan** (Moving Dirt) they were saying that our Earth Body, all of the Animal Nation, is a walking miracle. We are walking dirt. When we go back to Mother Earth we turn back into dirt.

And there are 3 more directions:
> Fifth Direction is up (blue), representing Creator, a Higher Power, God as symbolizing the sky/cosmos/universe, and goes by two names, **Wanbli Gleska** and **Tunkasila**, as a reference to God who is accepted as a grandfather.
>
> Sixth direction is down (green or brown), representing Mother Earth, **Ina Maka**, symbolizing the mother of all living energy and giver of life from below.
>
> The 7th direction is at the Center of your circle (purple), inside of you, symbolizing all of the Spirit-based teachings and wisdom of our elders who have passed on; it's God's energy inside you. This direction is one of the most important for maintaining balance and harmony with all the others.

Prayers to the east and the west are daily reminders of our life and death. We were made aware of these before the **Canupa Wakan** (pipe ceremony) came to us. The teachings of the **Canku Luta** (the red road or balance and harmony a two-legged has to walk on) runs from the south to the north.

The history books refer to the Sioux Uprising of 1862. The estimated 1,600 people (mostly families), who were not among the 38+2 killed by President Lincoln, were imprisoned at Fort Snelling, Minnesota, for two years after the hangings. The 38+2 refers to the 38 men who were hanged and the 2 additional chiefs who were kidnapped from Canada, returned to Fort Snelling, and then executed in front of the prisoners. During that time, the prisoners were treated horribly, and then taken by boat to Fort Thompson, South Dakota. Half of them were dropped off there, and the other half were taken to Santee, Nebraska. There were many deaths along the way, especially children, many of whom were put into the Missouri River without proper burial.

Because the Black Hills were taken away from us illegally with the violation of treaties and international human rights laws, and we were forced onto Reservations, we had no place to put our dead. The gold diggers just kept coming to the Black Hills and the government let them do it, so they kept us away from there, using guns to keep us on the Reservation, like prisoners. Since there was no place to put the dead, our people began to release them into the Missouri River. That's why grandmas look at the river as a graveyard.

The **Wacicu** (White, or White People) companies and corporations were trying to put hydroelectric lines and other energy projects on that land. The grandmas didn't want them to desecrate the burial grounds and were protesting about this in 2013. Before Europeans arrived, the oil pipelines were foreseen by our ancestors as a "Black Snake" that was coming to the people, a sickness that would disrupt balance and harmony. Our grandmas protested the Black Snake, too, and still do today.

Our people know that the Black Hills are sacred. Something not from this world created energy places there that are **Tiopas** (doorways) to God that are not man-made. This is why it is so heartbreaking and spiritually traumatic when non-Indians come digging around sacred lands and totally disrupt and disrespect our connection to God.

For non-Indians, you need to walk a mile in our moccasins to understand what we went through. We can't go through your graveyards and dig up the bones of your grandparents. How would you like that?

Without these sacred places, people have nowhere to release so they may heal.

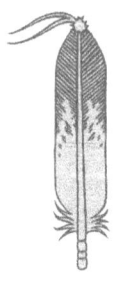

Wicokuja Sica
(Sickness to the Spirit, Mind, and Body)

The Impact of Catholicism on WoLakota

From John Collier, 1947

> *They had what the world has lost. They have it now. What the world has lost, the world must have again, lest it die. Not many years are left to have or have not, to recapture the lost ingredient. This is not merely a passing reference to World War III or the atom bomb—although the reference includes these ways of death, too. These deaths will mean the end if they come—racial death, self-inflicted because we have lost the way, and the power to live is dead. What, in our human world, is this power to live? It is the ancient, lost reverence and passion for human personality, joined with the ancient, lost reverence and passion for the earth and its web of life. This invisible reverence and passion is what the American Indians almost universally had; and representative groups of them have it still.*

They had and have this power for living, which our modern world has lost—as world-view and self-view, as tradition and institution.

By virtue of this power, the densely populated Inca state, by universal agreement among its people, made the conservation and increase of the earth's resources its foundational national policy. Never before, never since, has a nation done what the Inca state did. If our modern world should be able to recapture this power, the earth's natural resources and web of life would not be irrevocably wasted within the twentieth century, which is the prospect now. True democracy, founded in neighborhoods and reaching over the world, would become the realized heaven on earth. And living peace—not just an interlude between wars—would be born and would last through the ages.

Europeans fooled us. They came to us dressed like religious pilgrims carrying crosses with good intent, and then they killed us. When we met the European aliens that's one thing we observed about them. When they first came, they wore a mask with a smile on it, and we welcomed them with love. We always had an open-door way of life for all living things. That was a sign of generosity. Even today there are no doors on tipis. Once the Europeans found out about our way of life, they removed their masks and showed who they really were. That hurt us more than anything because they hurt us spiritually. It makes you spiritually weak. That is the worst trauma, when someone you love turns on you. It creates a spiritual wound that is really hard to heal. For those people who killed our family members, we will never forget it. It's in our DNA. The ones who have no feelings expect us to forget it. We can't!

Before the White man came, the Lakota practiced one religion. This one religion was Spirit-based and was lived twenty-four hours a day. There was so much respect for each other, they called each other by relative or they **Hunka** (adopted) each other because of the respect for the Circle of Life. Back then, people knew that everything is related to each other.

Ina Maka (Mother Earth) was respected as a Mother for her sustenance of life and her ***pejuta*** (medicine) to survive and live. All life survived on ***Ina Maka***, the plant life, the animals, the rocks, the water, the winged one, the ones who crawl, and the ones living in the water. ***Ina Maka*** will accept your body when you go to the Spirit World. The 4 directions are grandfathers and they represent Nations. The Wind is also a grandfather.

The respect for ***Taku Wakan Skan-Skan*** (something holy that has movement) is because everything has holiness and sacredness.

The sun is respected as ***Ate*** (Father) to give energy to everything that lives and grows.

The translators who interpreted Lakota into English did not do a good job. One of our Kul Wicasa Chiefs has several pictures. In one picture the translation says "Holy Bull," and in another picture the translation says "Medicine Bull." The translators were mixed-blood Lakota who misinterpreted words, sometimes out of humor, and would use misinterpretations that were vulgar. A lot of the names came from honor or were spiritual, like *Carries the Pipe, First Eagle, Circle Eagle, Hehaka Nunpa Pejuta,* and *Carries the Fire*. No one had disrespectful names. Only when the translators did this, did the names become disrespectful, by making fun of the names of our people.

My grandfather on my mother's side had three names: ***Carries the Fire*** (spiritual), ***Runs Close to Village*** (achievement for bravery), and ***Let Them Have Enough*** (honor and generosity). When the government census workers came and put our grandmother and grandfather's names in a tiny box, they butchered them. They drew my grandfather's first name out of a hat for boys and his name became Silas Fire, because *Carries the Fire* was too long for that little box. The older names, to my recollection, were astrological, which further supports that we are Star Beings. My grandfather's name was ***Wicahpi*** (star) ***Tanka*** (wise or physically big or bright). There are a lot of star names, like ***One Star, Two Stars, Morning Star***, and ***Sky Walker***.

Just kidding about Sky Walker! [*Laughter*] We have the story of the 7 sisters who married 7-star people, which leads to the story of my mom. One day my mom just collapsed. We all surrounded her, and relatives said, "Give her air!" I went outside and started crying. I looked up at the stars and I saw all these clear bright shiny stars. I said, "If there is a God up there, I want my mom to live." There was one star brighter than the others. I put my hands on my head and my elbows were on the log cabin. Suddenly, there was an energy standing next to me.

I'm going to use a movie because that's what it looked like. The movie was called *Terminator*. Arnold Schwarzenegger acted in that movie. In part two he comes back, and he helps guard this little boy from the Predator, who is trying to kill the boy who will become a scientist. The energy I saw was all silver like a liquid body. Just like the Predator. He asked me, "What's wrong?" I said, "I want my mom to live." Then I put my head back on my hands. When I looked back, he was gone. I was 9. My mom lived for a long time. That was one of my Star Relative experiences. After my mom passed on and they buried her, I got newspaper clippings for one whole week after. UFO activity was reported by the local farmers, and the police investigated many sightings of many lights where she was buried at Red Leaf. She was a *Star Woman*.

The early missionaries said, "You people pray to the devil, you are heathens and are wicked." Our elders who survived the missionaries' boarding schools were whipped and beaten into learning English and Christianity. Some of the beatings by the missionaries were very brutal, and that trauma has impacted many generations.

In the days of boarding schools, the government agents and the missionaries would shave children's hair off and put DDT on their heads to kill lice. They just lined them up and exposed them to chemicals, whether they had lice nits or not. This was introduced into our genetic bodies, exposure to DDT is bad like Agent Orange; DDT is an insecticide that is toxic to the Animal Nation when swallowed or absorbed through the skin. What may be even worse is the cutting of our hair. In the Lakota belief system, the length of hair was our connection to God. The teachings of **Woawanglaka** (taking care of the spiritual energy) is why we don't cut our hair without a good reason. Hair length was highly respected spiritually as it showed our connection to God. From a spiritual perspective, the only time we cut our hair is when we lose a loved one. When a parent, sister, or brother died, we showed our grief to that relative that passed on by cutting our hair. We did this to show to **Tunkasila** the love and compassion we had for that relative. When they cut our people's hair in boarding schools, it broke a universal law, bringing us bad luck, which we call **Wakunza** (the calling for death). Since we only cut our hair when someone dies, it was as if we were calling for death to come. First, the U.S. government agents and missionaries violated our belief system, and then they doused us with DDT, creating spiritual and genetic wounds passed down to the next generations.

One may ask, "How come you Indians are alcoholics and cannot do anything for yourselves?" The aftermath of domination is that we live in an oppressed environment, and we are conditioned into the dependence on welfare by the government. A few succeeded and left the Reservation system. But many of our Lakota people still live in a holocaust of racism, poverty, and disease that impacts our lives daily.

When will the government and the missionaries admit their wrongdoing and make amends for what they have done, and are still doing to us today? Apologies need to be publicly made from Congress and the President of the United States of America. In the United States, the Senate passed a resolution for an official apology to Tribal people called the *Native American Apology Resolution*, which was signed by President Obama on December 19, 2009, and stated that the president "apologizes on behalf of the people of the United States to all Native Peoples for the many instances of violence, maltreatment, and neglect inflicted on Native peoples by the *citizens* of the United States." However, the signing of this official apology was closed to the media, and there was nothing public about it.

Just over a year prior, on June 11, 2008, the Prime Minister of Canada made a national public broadcast apology for the damage done to the First Nations people at the hands of the government and provided details of the government's role in the trauma with actionable steps for reconciliation and healing.

In 2016, the *Smithsonian* published an article on the five times in history that the U.S. officially apologized. Apologies were made for shielding a Nazi officer wanted for war crimes, the imprisonment of Japanese people during World War II, the overthrowing of the Kingdom of Hawaii, the Tuskegee experiment conducted on Black men, slavery, and Jim Crow laws. But the U.S. official apology, signed in private, apologizing to Indigenous peoples, the original peoples of this land, was not included in the article because it was never made public. What a shame!

After Canada's government admitted their wrong to First Nations people, officials began taking action to investigate the Catholic Church. This goes across the board for both countries now, although in the U.S. it took White people to come forward as victims before lawsuits were successful in bringing justice to priests who sexually abused children.

In 2004, a civil lawsuit called *Blue Cloud Abbey* went before the South Dakota Supreme Court. In this case, the suit was against the Catholic Church for knowingly allowing the abuse of Indigenous children during their time at boarding school. As the case was in progress, the South Dakota legislature got involved and added to the statute of limitations. This law change resulted in limits of when a lawsuit could be filed: up to three years after a person remembers the abuse, and only up to age 40. The attorneys arguing the case said there should be "protection" for third-party groups, like the Catholic Church. The lawsuit was dismissed. There are many other stories like this, where no justice came for our Indigenous peoples. Now, as White people are coming forward saying they were abused, justice is being done. How can that be? Justice for one but not justice for all.

When Reservations were first developed, the early missionaries and the government agents enforced Christianity. If Indigenous people did not obey, we were labeled insane and were sent off to jail, then to the insane asylums, where we became a "white rat" to be practiced on by medical practitioners for the latest brain control methods. The majority of patients were normal and were strong, spiritual people who did not want to change and become like a White man.

If we obeyed and followed the rules, we saw the good-Spirit side of the early missionary workers. If we were "bad" and rebelled, we saw their bad side—evil—and felt the pain of the beatings and the punishment. Many children died and were secretly buried, and family members were told they fell off the stairs or some other accidental death was named. Families were also told that the youth had run away.

Recently, the Rosebud Treaty Council was discussing how to get the remains returned from boarding school youth that had died, many by murder and neglect. At one boarding school, a teacher was out in the marsh with students conducting science projects, and they uncovered bones. Many of these remains were from the youth who had been reported missing as runaways, yet these bones showed broken ribs, bullet holes in the head, and other inflicted wounds. Elders report that children died in the wetlands when running away, and that others were thrown there after they'd been murdered and reported as runaways by school officials.

Today elders are beginning to speak out with pain and anger against the assailants who traumatized their lives. My mother was a strong Christian and put me in an Episcopal boarding school when my father died. My father believed in our pipe way of life and taught me a lot of ceremonies from **Woptuga's** altar, my **Tunkasila** (Grandfather) "Buffalo Horn Chips." My mother, sisters, and brothers were products of boarding schools practicing military standards.

The majority of our people who experienced "boarding school," whether it was a government or a Christian one, were stigmatized for life. If you were a good product and followed the rules, you became a good "soldier"; you followed rules well, so they helped you. "Class pet" is an example of White ways. If you disobeyed, you were labeled "bad" and were treated as an "untrustworthy" person.

The sad part of all this is that when we begin to believe that we are "bad," we cannot succeed. So, when you have children, you beat them to be better than you, but this only increases and sustains the trauma. A large number of the victims of abuse have become severe alcoholics and drug users. Boarding schools did not teach the parenting skills of nurturing love and hugs that are seen in happy families.

Instead, we were just like a garden vegetable at a county fair: they showed us off to their peers, thrilled at how they changed us from heathen savages to civilized Christians. Of course, they did not show off the scars received physically, mentally, and spiritually, or the abuse our assailants rained down on us.

On September 12, 1985, when I made my commitment to live the life the Creator gave me and walk my spiritual path, I decided to let my Christian belief go and follow my **Tunkasila's** teachings. In order for me to stay strong, I gave of myself 100 percent, body-mind-soul, physically, mentally, spiritually, and used my Lakota values of Bravery, Generosity, Fortitude, and Wisdom (**Woohitika, Wacanteognaka, Wowacintanka, and Woksape**). I want to go where my grandparents of long ago went spiritually.

Many people all over the world have died in the name of Christianity. My people, the Red people, have also suffered with each greedy explorer who touched our land with their search for gold. But when your body has become a *dead battery*, you look for a place to *charge up*.

It is like looking for God—**Tunkasila.** We don't have to look all around the world. "Spirit" is inside of us, brothers and sisters. **Tunkasila** is in you, look inside yourself. The most important direction, the 7th Direction.

Our people, all over **Ina Maka** (Mother Earth) must go through healing.

We must replace anger, fear, and intimidation, with the positives of harmony, peace, and love.

If ***Tunkasila*** (Creator) told us we were made from ***Ina Maka*** and that our Earth Body would return and seep back into Mother Earth, then we are not different from each other.

Does our Spirit have color, and is there a White Spirit World, Red Spirit World, Black Spirit World, and Yellow Spirit World? I believe there is not!

Our spiritual practitioners who do not walk-the-talk all over the world create divisions and barriers, excluding people and even dehumanizing them.

I see it today in Indian Country, and also abroad, where groups are forming and following a Spirit leader who proclaims their work to be holy and sacred, or say that their way is the only true way. Some say, "I am more ***Wakan*** (sacred/holy) because I pray with so and so," or "I am more ***Wakan*** because I pray like this."

What is ***Wakan*** is to use unconditional love as a guiding force in your life and the way you treat others. ***Waunsila*** *is to have pity for one another*. This sacred, Spirit-based universal law of having pity for one another is strong, a bonding of family, no matter who you are. It is part of the ***Wamakaskan*** (Animal Nation). Even animals have pity for one another. We must have pity on one another, as Christians and Lakotas, and those who practice both.

Today, our Indigenous children are being taken from their families because of immigration policy. They are denied religious freedom in schools, incarcerated at higher rates in federal jails and prisons, and are still more likely to be placed into foster care with White families, many of whom unconsciously continue to assimilate them into a White Christian worldview. Indigenous youth around the globe are plagued with the disparities of despair that come from living on remote reserves impacted by climate change, being restricted from accessing sacred spiritual lands, and living with ongoing historical and intergenerational trauma with little opportunity to get out. Now our Indigenous youth are more likely to end their life than any other group of youth around the globe. Many of our youth would rather kill themselves than live in the world that the Christian immigrants and colonizers created for them.

Historically, European Christians have called us unholy to convince people to turn away from us. Indians were called savages, even though we cared for Europeans with compassion when they arrived here. Today, Mexicans crossing the border are called dirty, though they are mostly Indigenous families who have more right to be on Turtle Island[1] than anyone of European descent, as this land is also their original homeland, and we have been engaging Nation to Nation for thousands of years already. Muslims are called terrorists, even when the vast majority of them are kind, caring, peaceful people. You get the point.

After the Catholics and Christians[2] called—and often still call—us unholy and people turn away from us, the discrimination follows. Hangings, lynchings, incarceration, stealing children, denying jobs, denying housing, and the rest of the bad things follow.

From a Lakota belief, when a man kills his own people that is very dishonorable. Where did that teaching come from for the Europeans? This teaching came out of greed.

When a man pollutes Mother Earth for his own gain, that is very selfish. Where did that teaching come from? It's called greed.

Who is the heathen? Who is the savage? Who has the horns and tail sitting there, holding their pitchfork? So many Indigenous people have died, and continue to die, not for religion, but for gold. Those in power use religion to push sadistic policies such as Indian Removal, Sundown, Lynching, and Reservations; and today, separating children from families and locking them up in cages at the border.

Those in power don't know when to stop and be happy. When will they stop?

---

1 Turtle Island is the original name of the lands of North America (Alaska, Canada, and the United States) but has also been used to include Central and South America. The term predates the colonial borders that separated us.

2 Only Catholics and Christians forced religion and historical traumas on Indigenous peoples of Turtle Island. Even today Jewish people are not trying to convert Indigenous people to Judaism, and because of their own historical trauma we have a common understanding.

Woniyan Woeihunble
Dreams That Give Life

*T*HREE DREAMS CAME TO ME when I was 17. At first, I accepted these dreams. I kept dreaming about the same things over and over again. Then those three dreams started coming back when I was 21.

After I sobered up in 1985, I was 32, and I finally took the dreams to a Medicine Man to have them interpreted. Then I wanted more clarity, so I went to another Medicine Man. In total, I went to 7 Medicine Men. I thought about all of the interpretations I heard. Grandfather was trying to tell me something I needed to do. The word **Wotawacin** (Blueprint) that I have been talking about kept coming to me. This relates to the Spirit talk. The Blueprint is our Spirit, like our DNA. These dreams were telling me to come home to work with our people so that we may *Return to Blueprint*, to help "reset" us to our pre-colonial gifts, talents, knowledge, and ways, so that we may connect with the Spirit World again.

I'm not supposed to be out there in the non-Indian world. The Medicine Men specifically said our youth are crying and are lost. They said, **Onuni** (our youth are lost) or **Omani** (our path is lost). In other words, no GPS!

As a result of intergenerational trauma, we lost the understanding of the word "love." In teaching how to love, you have to learn how to let go. The best way to let go spiritually is to cry. That's why when people hold back their tears and they finally open up, they cry really hard and you can hear them lose their breath. I've seen that in severe spankings of my relatives. They didn't spank me, but I cried so hard for them because there was so much trauma. When Lakota parents beat their children, it is a teaching from boarding school. How many of them experienced this type of treatment when that love connection was lost? What remains is hatred and anger towards those who beat us, and, in our minds, we have thoughts of revenge.

We then may take the path to alcohol and drugs because it's numbing. Maria Yellow Horse Brave Heart talks about the psychic numbing[3] where you can't react because your Spirit is frozen. They are all psychological terms that the common man struggles to understand. "When you talk to us common people," I told Dr. Brave Heart, "you should break down those words so we can understand them." She is a forerunner and leader to help our people understand what happened to us so that we may heal from the holocaust that occurred here. I thank her for this! Wopila!

I finally realized that we had to look at our people as a whole, know that our Nation is in recovery, and be aware of the open wounds that we are all trying to heal from. It upsets those of us who are educated if someone goes "Whoo, whoo, whoo, whoo" (stereotypical sounds people make while slapping their mouth in a very ridiculous attempt to lulu) or asks, "Where is your tipi?" They are not aware of the open wounds we have. These are triggers to the anger that our people have not completely put out. It's like an invisible bleeding scar.

I hear and see the Europeans call themselves a superior race throughout my life with their words and actions. I wonder, if they are a superior race, why have they taken so many people's lives in

---

3   The American Indian Holocaust, https://pubmed.ncbi.nlm.nih.gov/9842066/.

the name of greed? If you are superior, you let the energy of life go on because Grandfather/God made it. There is a reason and purpose why every living thing is alive. There is no respect for life if we abuse life-giving forces such as water and other energies. Europeans forced us to cut our umbilical cord to Mother Earth and now we are all abusing life, so much so that it's polluting our world now. So much sadness this abuse makes us all carry.

After consultation with 7 altars (Medicine Men), I knew I had to come home. When I did, I saw my own children feel a lot of suffering because they were not exposed to that type of trauma that the other youth in our community were being exposed to. They hadn't seen the "trauma drama" that is done in the homes today. When I brought them back home to the Reservation, they had a really hard time adjusting. My daughter would say there are so many bullies in the school. So much so, she would come home crying on the bus, so I drove them to school every day. I would be the only dad standing on the playground with all the kids, to observe my kids, to see how other kids treated them.

My son is Walks with the Energy of Two Elks. The Elks Energy is love. It's a love Spirit. My great-grandfather must have been a loving man. I was watching Tombstone with Doc Holiday and Wyatt Earp. Doc was in a saloon and they were drinking and playing a card game. He told those he was playing with that he was a loving man. The other man said, "Loving man, it's your turn." [Laughter]. My grandfather must have been a loving man because they gave him that name. My son is the ninth generation carrying that name. That's 540 years, if each generation lived to the age of 60. I'm 65. It's also before Columbus landed in America and thought he found the real "Indians." That's how long that Walks with the Energy of Two Elks (Walks with the Energy of Love That Is Greater Than One) has been around.

My theory is that our people were very loving. There was no domestic violence in the tipi. No violence against children. No abandoned children. Your whole Tribe was your family. There was so much love from the mom and dad that the aunties and uncles would discipline the kids. I couldn't be mean to my kids, because it would hurt me. Gentle teaching, they call it. You raise them in a gentle way. The idea of shaking, slapping, and other forms of physical abuse came from religious boarding schools. One of my uncles gave me advice. He said that anytime we boys had a problem with his wife or other women, we just needed to abuse them to straighten them out. He was raised by a boarding school. He is the product of boarding school. The cure-all was to beat your wife to get her back in line. I saw enough of that growing up! I saw enough of my relatives and friends getting beat up by their husbands.

In one of the recurring dreams, it always starts off where I am a human being, but I am small like an ant and floating on a big leaf. I am standing on a leaf floating on water. It is dark with a little light off in the distance. As I look around, the leaf bumps into these huge roots of huge trees as they gravitate toward that light. As I approach the light, I see a lodge that looks like our Sweat Lodge, but it is canvas. It is round and covered with hides. There is a door on the lodge, and it is situated on a beach. There is a lit fire burning with flames. My leaf gets closer and closer and there are no other human beings or animals around. As I get closer the leaf docks on the beach. I get off the leaf and I walk toward the fire. This grandfather comes out of the lodge, and he is carrying two sacred pipes. In one hand the pipe bowl is black, and in the other hand the pipe bowl is red. And he walks towards me. I look at him and he offers both pipes. He does not say anything. It is either the black pipe or the red pipe. After looking at him for a while, and before I can choose, he turns and walks back into the lodge with the pipes. And just as I get back on the leaf, I wake up.

In the second dream, again, I'm floating on something in some water and it's dark and I bump into something like a beach but it's all rocks, round boulders. There is a light from above the rocks. I begin to climb these rocks to the light. When I get to the light, there is a hole and I peek out. I crawl out of the hole and onto this earth. I'm in the graveyard. I hear a car not too far away that's stuck, and I hear voices. I come out of the ground and walk towards the car. It is a 1940s model, like a coupe. There are men who are wearing long coats that go down below their knees. They are wearing hats like Dick Tracy's. The collars of their coats are up so I can't see their faces. Same with the women: they have long coats and are wearing scarves on their heads that cover their faces. I help them push the car out of the gate of the graveyard. I help them push it, and then I wake up.

In the third dream, I am on one side of the river where there is no vegetation. It's all sand. There is this blue river about 40- to 50-feet wide, and across the river is green grass. Everything is green with flowers. There are elder men and women in buckskin clothing, and they are playing a game with a ball. It is like croquet. It is a very gentle game. They all have white hair, men and women, wearing braids. A voice says, "Look at the ball." When I look at it, I can see it is Mother Earth. Far beyond these elders playing that game on the green grass is a huge shade tree, like an oak tree. You can hear birds there. Beyond that are rolling hills, and beyond that I can hear lots of kids having lots of fun, like they are at the carnival. I can't see them, I can only hear them. Inside of myself, my Spirit wants to cross the river, pass the elders, fly over the tree to the place where the children are playing. I hear other voices on both sides of me. I see men, women, and children standing on both sides of me as far as the eye can see, and they are either holding a marijuana joint or a drug or alcoholic beverage, just like I am. We are all standing along the river where there is no life or vegetation growing, and we are saying, "Don't drink, don't drug."

One of the interpretations that I received is that water is the gift of life. I need to go through this process of purification, cleansing. At one point, I feel like I am halfway across the water now. There is no time limit. Maybe I am supposed to get to the elders who are playing with Mother Earth. I was told it was not grandma and grandpa but wisdom that is helping to guide the energy of life on Mother Earth. That huge tree is a symbol of Grandfather. And those voices and the laughter are the Spirits that are not physical yet, where this is a lot of joy. It brings tears to my eyes hearing all of those kids play. Then I wake up.

Those are recurring dreams that have no completion. I wonder why just those three dreams keep coming back. They don't go forward, they don't have a beginning or a happily-ever-after ending.

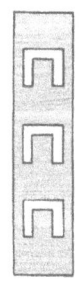

— PART 1 —

Wowakan Kicopi
(THE CALLING)

Wicokuja
(SICKNESS OF THE PEOPLE) THAT AFFECTS THE *Canupa Wakan* (SACRED ENERGY)

The Good and the Bad, the Yin and the Yang

I'M GOING TO TELL YOU about a historical event. The world was having chaos and a savior came to Mother Earth to realign the teachings of God. For the Muslims, it was Mohammed, for the Christians, it was Jesus. It's ironic that Jesus was trying to tell them that he was the Son of God, but they didn't believe him. Then they killed him and a big surge of Christianity came about. They made him a martyr.

About the same time, the White Buffalo Calf Woman came to save our people, the Lakota, because we were getting out of balance too. She was the savior of the Dakota, Lakota, and Nakota people. The White Buffalo Calf Woman brought the ***Canupa Wakan***, with teachings for us to follow to find our balance and harmony.

She brought 4 sacred rights and three were to follow after her, for a total of 7. The three that followed would come through dreams to Medicine Men. These dreams were made specifically for men. God spoke through the Medicine Men to tell them that the **Wicokuja** (negative energy) was coming, that the Europeans were coming and that our blood would be on their hands.

For us, we have our own creation story, and the White Buffalo Calf Woman came to reinforce the sacred teachings of the **Wakan** (sacred) energy. As it happened, two **Tokalas** (men who spread blue energy) were hunting buffalo, and they came upon a woman carrying a bundle. As they approached her, one had evil thoughts about her, and she motioned him to come forward. As he came forward and stood in front of her, there was a cloud of smoke, and when it lifted, the man was transformed to bones. This is a clear example of negative energy and what happens when you come in contact with the power of the sacred. Negativity is not allowed around our sacred ceremonies and negative energy impacts the power of the sacred teachings. The good Tokala, who did not have evil thoughts and respected her as **Wakan** (holy), was given a message to take back to the Lakota **Oyate.** The message was that she was going to bring the sacred bundle to the people, and he was to tell the people when she was coming.

The White Buffalo Calf Woman teaches us about the good and the bad, like the Yin and the Yang that the Chinese speak of. Ever since then, when positive energy goes up so does negative energy. Every time there is an attempt of good energy, bad energy tries to match it. We see this across all of our cultures.

Today, the good **Tokala** are dying, and the bad men that were reduced to bones are slowly coming back to life, carrying the medicine of **Wicokuja** (bad, unhealthy, or unnatural energy).

My uncle was asked to pray at one of our many Sundance ceremonies, but after he learned that 7 Bad Men were planning to run the Sundance, he refused. He said *"**Wiwan yung wacipi Hocokan tab ki asabyab**."* ("The negative people who are playing with our Sacred Pipe at a Sacred Sundance, nothing good will come out of it. They are darkening the circle.) The messenger went back to the 7 bad men and told them that the uncle refused. The 7 bad men called my uncle every bad name in the book and they continued to hold the Sundance. It reminded me of a band of pirates trying to run a sacred Lakota ceremony.

Black Elk, in his book, *Black Elk Speaks*, says: "The bad cannot see or touch the sacred pipe." What I observe is that they can touch the sacred pipe physically, but nothing spiritually will work for them.

Wowakan (Sacred Energy)

The term ***Wowakan*** is a universal law that all energy is sacred. ***Wowakan*** was respected before the arrival of the Europeans. The 4th direction that we pray for is the Animal Nation. The understanding of ***Wowakan*** is that we all come from that family of the Animal Nation. When we put the 7 pinches of red willow in our pipe bowl, the Animal Nation is the 4th pinch. To understand the teachings that we come from the dirt—from Mother Earth—and that our Earth Body—when it comes back to Mother Earth—will turn back to dirt, helps reinforce the creation stories. For Lakota, ***Inyan*** created Mother Earth so that she would be a giver for all living energy that is here on earth. ***Wowakan*** is a teaching we all grew up with before European contact. With that understanding, ***Mitakuye Oyasin*** (All my relatives), we know all living energy. Not only the Animal Nation, but also the living energy of the wind, the water, the sun, the plants, the rocks, the moon. Oh yeah, and the stars! We not only have our nuclear family, but we have a universal family. I listened to stories of grandpas and grandmas and how they could communicate to this living energy. The water can talk. The wind can talk. Every living energy has a voice, including all of the animal world. If you were alive during that time and experienced this, it was a very harmonious way of life to be able to communicate with all living energy. We were always with our family no matter where we went.

Since 1986, I've been going to Bear Butte, fasting and praying, and in 1991, I met a Star Relative there. I don't ask to be a holy sacred man. I only go there to give prayers of thanksgiving and prayers for protection for the next year. I have a lot of respect for holy men. I met a Being at Bear Butte who is not from this world. When I saw the Being, it startled me that the Star Relatives can manifest in the physical. It created an irregular heartbeat in me, from the shock. When there is extreme shock, it affects your health in some way. That's why I like the movie *Star Wars* because in it Luke Skywalker and all these other guys go to these other planet rest areas for other starships, like Space Stations, to stop in and eat or whatever. In one scene there is a bar and you see all of the strange interplanetary people socializing, and they don't look the same. That's like our Star Relatives.

At one time, there was a race of Star Relatives that came to Mother Earth; they have skin like reptiles. When they came, they created reptiles here. Earth was visited by many of these Space Relatives that come from different races or types of Star Relatives. Intelligent beings do not try to dominate or destroy each other. They have the technology to exterminate us already, but they do not. That energy of love and compassion comes from an intelligent being. That's why we are still here.

My brother, Dr. A. C. Ross, found in his research that out there near the Pleiades, there is a planet called Lyra, which he believes is where Star People found on earth may have originated. He told me how there are many graves being opened in Arizona where huge skeletons were being found of 12- to 15-feet tall people. There used to be giants on Mother Earth. The Bible talks about Goliath, the giant who walked the earth. Where did the giants go? This planet was visited by Space People before.

There is an archeological term called earthworks, which basically refers to artificial archeological features on earth. Tribal mounds are also considered earthworks along with other unexplained archeological wonders, such as the Nazca lines in Peru. There is a theory that many of these features represent Sundance circles of those who visited here before. There was something that had a lot of power that was here before and left. There is something **Wakan** (sacred) in the middle of that circle. It's almost like they felt an interruption that was coming that was not going to be helpful for them, so they took that energy west to flee from it. What followed was conversion and baptism. Anyone not baptized was not considered human. We helped Europeans live when they landed on the eastern shores of our lands. They called it Thanksgiving. Our turkey. Some non-Indian said on the radio, "We should be thankful to the Native Americans because they helped our ancestors survive here that first year." The Star People left before they could be baptized.

What they left behind, the earthworks, are like portals that connect us to the other world. Our connection has gone underground, but a new Sacred Energy is coming.

Dr. Ross believes that these beings could dematerialize and then materialize again in another place, much like our ancestors. Grandpa Fools Crow talked about Medicine Men who, as late as the 1800s, could disappear and reappear 20 to 30 feet away, because of their purity. One of my uncles talked about our grandpa who had the ability to fly from one place to the other. They didn't see him flying. Others said his body would appear and disappear. He had a Spirit that could travel—they travel in their Spirit and then materialize when they get there. A lot of that stuff is like Star Wars. Dr. Ross uses books to describe this process, and I know he is right because I can use my own experiences to tell you. This travel can span dimensions and worlds for both our Star Relatives manifesting on other planets and our Spirit Relatives who may remain stuck here on earth.

Remember the movie *Ghost* when he meets the other Spirit in the subway and that Spirit doesn't want him to be in that subway? When you are alive on Mother Earth and you are very greedy your energy doesn't cross over. It remains in certain areas. The other ghost energy told Patrick Swayze to leave the subway and yelled, "This is mine!" That Spirit of greed and domination kicked him out of the subway because that energy is caught between worlds. Those people who are selfish, who are greedy, who don't want to leave their wealth or whatever, will still haunt places. Patrick Swayze stays on earth to find his killer, so he can have the justice to cross over. Some Spirits, like the one on the Subway, just want to remain where they are. They do not want to cross over.

I met a lot of people who have connections to Star Relatives. For me, when I was 17 years old and had my out-of-body experience, that is who I met. They were intergalactic, they were star walkers, and they would move in a blink of an eye. And that was me, too. I could go or do anything I wanted to do, and I could come back to my body or near my body.

In 1991 when I met a Star Relative, he (she or they) was a thin person wearing a gray uniform, and he had those officer belt loops that sat on top of his shoulders, and he was what looked like an old man with white hair, but when he got close I could see it was a white skull cap. I thought he was wearing dark glasses but those were his eyes. He had a tiny nose, small mouth, and normal head size but he was thin, real thin. We communicated without our lips moving and we were not talking. They have this ability to take you someplace for a certain period of time, and then they can bring you back 15 to 20 minutes before they took you—and you won't remember where you went.

A lot of our spiritual Medicine Men encountered Star Relatives and gave them Lakota names. They also gave a way for calling them, so that they could talk to you anytime, anyplace, wherever you go on Mother Earth. It doesn't come in a weak voice. It comes in a normal to loud voice. It's not language or words, but an understanding. It is a connection you have. That's why I studied sacred vibration because the ear doesn't catch a language, it catches a sacred vibration. Like the drum, it sends a sacred vibration to the brain and the brain creates the language.

I do believe that our ancestors, 300 years ago, didn't speak through verbal contact. I think we communicated to other Indigenous people through our minds, along with communicating with other animals. The belief is that our Earth Body came from dirt, but our Spirit Body came from another place. All religions have this belief of coming from Mother Earth and being made from dirt. Our bones come from rocks. If you look at our computers, they're made of rock, quartz. If you listen to these abductees who tell their story, they say they have been implanted with something and they go through surgery to get it removed. And it is usually a rock.

Our medicine people, when they were calling these relatives, they befriended them and gave them Lakota names. One of our Star Relatives is called *The One Who Walks With Good Life*. He does a lot of Star Travel. Star Relatives can be as small as a virus or a germ, but also so big that they can hold Mother Earth between their fingers like a BB pellet. I'll save that part for another time and another book.

Your connection to the Spirit World is like tuning into the radio. You can tune it in like you do to a radio channel.

I understand that Bear Butte is a sacred place where we communicate with relatives from the stars. The Star Relatives will only visit us when we glow. When we glow is when we have worked on ourselves, let go of the negative energy, and have achieved spiritual purity. Then we are at the level of our Star Relatives, a level of purity. Our Star Relatives had some type of power that created travel in a blink. For me, to become more aware of that is to partake in a ceremony called Vision Quest. In Lakota Vision Quest you become aware of all these things that grandpas and grandmas used to talk about. Through dream interpretation you begin to know what kind of spiritual being you are in this world. This creates the respect for yourself and others who walk with altars that have the ability to communicate with **Tunkasila**, and shows how you must sustain this good energy for the rest of your life. For all of the time you are here in the physical world.

I believe there were spiritual helpers we tuned into who helped our people do superhuman things. An example is when my great-grandmother, Earth Nation Woman, saved five grandchildren, including my grandpa, Robert Two Elk, from the Wounded Knee butchering. She saved them and, overnight, they escaped.

Within this experience there is a fear factor called **Wonihinciya** (spiritual fear of the Spirit, the mind, or the body; or holistic fear that affects the mind and the body). In the old days we called White people **Mila Hunska** (Long Knives) because of the terror they invoked upon our people. The Long Knives were a description of the swords the colonizers used to decapitate our people. This didn't just happen to the Lakota people. In the documentary, *Doctrine of Discovery*,[4] there is a story about how the Spaniards murdered Indigenous people from the south in their sleep. These colonizers were bragging about how they could split an Indigenous person in half with one swoop of the sword, and how quickly they could kill a baby by bashing its head on a rock. The next day they cut the limbs to the elbows of the survivors and told them to go into the mountains to spread the word to those who ran away that this is what would happen to them if they didn't pay taxes to the Spanish priest. Near the same time, the British murdered the Lenape Tribe in Manhattan in the same fashion. You can see the conflict this might create, when learning that a priest or religious entity, who one would think should have positive energy, is the one behind the terror being inflicted on Indigenous peoples.

The body response is fight or flight. Let's say the cavalry comes riding into a peaceful camp before we knew they were Long Knives who caused us fear. At first, there may be a physical fear and we believe there is a possibility of surviving, but when we start seeing our people being beheaded, we go into mental and spiritual

---

4   *Doctrine of Discovery, Unmasking the Domination Code* (2014), https://meaningfulmovies.org/events/the-doctrine-of-discovery-unmasking-the-domination-code

fear because death is imminent. The multigenerational survivors of Wounded Knee are always looking over our shoulders, and we pass this on to our children and grandchildren through the expression of our DNA, through our blood. A mind's response is the possibility of survival, the inability to think, and the possibility of death. The mind would react to the fear of death when one sees the butchering of its own people.

There is a reason why my grandpa survived that massacre. If he didn't survive, he wouldn't have my father and my father wouldn't have me and I wouldn't have my son. I am the message of that Sacred Energy that our people once had. In my family that was almost wiped out because, paternally, I am the only one who now carries that wisdom until my son is ready to receive this wisdom as medicine to help us live. That is the purity, the survival. My grandpa survived for me and for those coming after me.

I heard from an uncle about stories when he was little about our people doing time and space travel. He would say that relatives would go to grandma's country (Canada) by traveling all night, walking. The next day, they would arrive in Sioux Valley, Canada. When I would drive from Rosebud to Sioux Valley, it would take me 12 hours, one way, at 60 mph. That's how fast they could travel. How did they do that?

My uncle, who is a Medicine Man, told a story of a grandpa who was also a Medicine Man before the horse (Sacred Dog) came to our people. He talked about how my grandpa would be called to help those who were sick, and he would show up out of thin air. After 4 days of doctoring, when he was called upon to go to another place, he would leave a small leather shaped bird with the family and tell them if their relative started to get sick again to put the bird outside the tipi, and the bird would come and get him. When their relative person got sick again, the family would put the bird outside of the tipi; it would come to life and fly away. Shortly after, my grandpa would show up. That's pure energy. That's what you call spiritual purity.

Taku Wakan Skan Skan (something holy or sacred that has movement).

Wowakan (sacred or spiritual energy) is universal law. It's an ongoing cycle of life here on Mother Earth. Mother Earth has cleansed herself three times. Today in the chaos that we are living in, the elders know it is time for the 4th cleansing. After the 4th cleansing, we will have peace again. In any crisis situation, life starts over after the crisis ends. How can we—as a ***Hunupa*** or a *two-legged*—how can we be part of the healing that needs to take place for the 7th generation and for Mother Earth? How can we be on the side of ***Wowakan*** or *Sacred Energy*?

Watohun Oko Wan Pima Oiyokipi Pejuta Tunkasila Unkupi
THE MEDICINE OF HUMOR

On the third day of Sundance is a day of prayer and healing with the tree. All of the dancers had been preparing for a year. Some had brought little ones to the tree to share spiritual grounding. I believe that when the Spirit comes into this world it is like a baptism to introduce the Spirit to the symbol of the Creator. And so on this beautiful, respectful day, everyone who came was asking for healing. The sun dancers who were praying at the tree invited the people to come and pray with them. Following this prayer was a dance. All of my relatives sitting under the arbors were respectfully attentive. I was standing in the center of the circle facing the South. When I lifted my arms up to pray, I felt cool air blowing on my legs and everyone burst out laughing because my skirt had fallen all the way down to my ankles. At that moment, all of that sacredness disappeared, and the medicine of laughter took over. It felt so good for all of us to laugh. It is a good thing I had long underwear.

The moral to this story is that one of our medicines is humor. Life is to be enjoyed, not be so serious all the time. To let go of anger, and realize that **Tunkasila** does this to make us lighten up and laugh at ourselves, so we can bring that essence of laughter. Every once in a while the medicine of laughter comes through this **Oko** (crack or opening) and into this world. Humor comes into our mind and body when we least expect it. It comes to us to make us laugh. To this day my fellow dancers and relatives tease me and ask if I still have teddy bears on my underwear.

Negi Makoce Etan Unhipi
(WE COME FROM THE SPIRIT WORLD)

*L*AKOTA LIFE IS SPIRIT BASED, meaning that 200 years ago, and even further back, we communed 24 hours a day with our ***Tunkasilas*** (Grandfathers). We referred to God as our own Grandfather. This same grandfather's energy or movement is in the trees, water, fire, rocks, and the 4 directions that have the ability to give life or take life. We also respect the Earth as our mother; lifegiver. Some refer to her as ***Unci*** (Grandmother) because of her time and age. We look at everything around us, above us, below us, as a relative. We have read and have been told of the 6 directions, but the most important direction is the 7th direction—ourselves.

In my personal experience of my relatives who were Medicine Men, they considered themselves a filter. Grandpa Fools Crow used to say, "I am just a hollow bone." We carry this Spirit energy, which includes our collective unconsciousness, through our ***We(h)*** (blood). Over time, we assimilated into what is called a "comfort zone," where fewer Indian lifestyles have been accepted by the White society as a "Good Indian." The system changed our attitude and personality by reinforcing us to be less Indian and more White. It has created shame to be Indian or part Indian.

You are more accepted by the White society if you are less Indian, having names like Jack and Jill. The less you know/are, the better you feel.

Inside my **Hocoka**, my circle, no one speaks English. That's where I go, so I can feel comfortable and keep my knowledge strong with our teachings. In my six years of church school I never felt like a Christian. Maybe because I wasn't raised that way. I was raised with our spiritual grounding and awareness of Mother Earth, Father Sun, the greater galaxy and the invisible world of the sacred energy of our family.

Today there is a reawakening of this sleeping giant called by mainstream, the American Indian, which for me is the great Lakota Nation and the even greater Oceti Sakowin Oyate, representing one fire of the Dakota, Lakota, and Nakota peoples. Lakota elders have spoken of the "Mending of the Sacred Hoop" by the 7th generation. We must all move in that direction to help this grow. ***Hecel oyate ki wicohun na wicoiye waste ki tan woableza yuha manib ktelo*** (Our people can walk with this knowledge toward the future).

Our children's behavior is the outcome of our physical, mental, and spiritual scars that we carry as a once proud Lakota Nation. It brings tears to my eyes when I think of the traumas that our grandfathers and grandmothers went through and what they hung on to, our Spirit-based knowledge. They kept this knowledge so that our people may live with the Creator through the White Buffalo Calf Woman gift of the Sacred Pipe (**Canupa Wakan**) and its universal laws, the 7 sacred rites.

Today, as soon as someone mentions **Canupa Wakan** (Sacred Pipe), many stop paying attention. Ask yourself, what makes you not want to listen or pay attention? Is it the comfort zone? There is an invisible world that we came from called **Nagi** (Spirit). Understanding cannot come when we move away spiritually, mentally, and physically.

To understand the invisible world we came from, we must first understand that the woman is the host to receive the Spirit energy into this world. Birthing is a ceremony that comes with proper grounding and love. That word love is very important. Once a woman knows she is carrying another energy and there is movement in her womb, mother and father are both very happy as there is a gift coming from the Creator. From the Spirit World. A woman has more Spiritual power than a man because women go through the longest ceremony of carrying a new energy coming to Mother Earth. That ceremony takes 9 months of **Wokakija**, or mental, physical, and Spiritual suffering. There is a communion that occurs with the Woman and Creator as she is hosting the Spirit to come into the physical body, the Earth Body. She will create it with her womb.

The grounding energy of love is important for the child to have a normal birth. After a child is born, it is critical for the Spirit, the body, and the mind to have no interruptions in grounding until the age of 2. An infant is connected to that Spirit World as long as there is a soft spot on top of the head. After that soft spot closes around the age of 2 years old, the Spirit can stay in the body. The entire responsibility for grounding is with the mother, as she is the host.

I went to a workshop with Ethleen Iron Cloud Two Dogs and my **Tahansi** (cousin) Rick Two Dogs. They had doctors there to collaborate on what they were saying. They talked about how, from the time of conception to 2 years old, if anything mentally, spiritually, or physically happens to the baby or the mom, it can damage the soul. The pregnant mom shouldn't even hear negative things. You need to have this grounding during that time in the womb from both mom and dad and the family. That grounding energy is love.

Understanding the process of being a human mother is the same as how we Lakota look at Mother Earth. We are born from our mother, and when we die our body goes back to dirt and our Spirit goes home to where we come from.

But when trauma happens in life, the Spirit can leave and get stuck outside of the body. It won't go far. It will stay near the body, but it's not inside the person because the Spirit wants to go home. In the world of psychology, they call it dissociation, which might include depersonalization (feeling as if the world is not real) or derealization, (feeling as if the self is not real), which creates the "out-of-body experience" that people talk about. That's why we have a Calling Back the Spirit ceremony, **Wicakicopi**, which can be conducted for a person of any age.

In order for the mind and body to be healthy, the mom and environment need to be healthy. We have ceremonies that go along with the birthing and child-rearing that are helpful for a healthy life on Mother Earth. The birthing process is really critical. For the mother, proper nutrition from Mother Earth in the form of plants, herbs, and animals will keep that child growing healthy while being created in her womb. Birthing is so important, I have much more to say about it, but understanding the ceremony must happen first.

Tobtopa
(The Teachings of The 4, 4, 4, 4)

Circle of Life

THERE ARE 4 QUARTERS to the physical Circle of Life. The first quarter is our Spirit coming into the world; the first quarter begins from the first breath we take until our first rite of passage at puberty. The second quarter of life is becoming an adult; it begins after the puberty rite of passage until we follow proper Lakota protocols to begin our own family. The third quarter of life is from the time we begin our own family until we reach the second rite of passage in elderhood, when menopause occurs, which happens for both men and women. The 4th quarter of life is from elderhood to death. Then the Circle of Life starts all over again.

There are also two stages in the spiritual Circle of Life. The first stage is pre-birth that occurs during the 9-month cycle. The second stage is post-death that lasts for 13 moons after you die.

From conception to birth we must rely on prayer to ask for a good Spirit to come into the family. This is also the first stage of the ceremony, which is known as Calling. There must be a commitment to nurture and love to help this Spirit grow in a positive way, when the Spirit enters this earthly life to live its 4 quarters of life. The first quarter of life is the **Wakanyeja** stage, when you have one foot in the door of the visible (physical) world. During this quarter the children are considered sacred or holy and are treated as such. The children are innocent and live on unconditional love. The teachings and knowledge come from the other three quarters of life; the young adult, the middle age, and the last age is the elder age—**Wakan** (sacred).

During the **Wakanyeja** (first quarter of life) of sacred children, stories were told that carried life values, both positive and negative outcomes for learning. Sacred children could prophesize in their behavior **Wakunza** (Spirit acting). Mothers and grandmothers always advised children in their play because of **Wakunza**. Because of their sacredness, if they played death and dying, they were advised not to because this is what they will bring to the family, Tribe, and Nation. When I was a kid we used to play in cardboard boxes when we went to town. The elder woman in my family would take the boxes away and would cut them up or burn them because they simulated death, like we were playing in a casket or a coffin.

I wonder how many of our sacred children play and make believe of alcohol situations, and violence? If you ever see a child make a gun out of their finger and pretend they are shooting it at you, that is Spirit acting. Children always imitate adults; they watch and act out adult situations. Are they predicting their future?

There is a sacred Lakota word—**Wowahokunkiya**—which is a universal law that means to give *spiritual advice or wisdom for survival* to our young. This was practiced by our elders. **Wowahokunkiya** is **Pejuta** (medicine) for our young to help them grow and be healthy, body-mind-Spirit.

Nagi Wi Cakicopi
(CALLING THE SPIRIT BACK) AND
Woistapakinta
(WIPING OF THE TEARS)

[The following was very difficult to complete, as we had to stop and start many times. This was during one of our phone sessions while I was home in Oklahoma and Tokala calling in from a community. I will not say which community out of respect for their privacy. At one point on the call, Tokala fell silent for a very long moment. It felt like an eternity, and I checked my phone to see if we were still connected. The seconds were still tracking on my phone so I remained silent with him. Then he said he could not continue today with our session, and he apologized. He had been at a school, helping youth and family members who were grieving the loss of a young person who died by suicide. I understand very well that, even though we are trained to respond to these kinds of crises, it is the most difficult task we ever face and there is always shock and pain for us too, the helpers . . . .]

I THINK, WELL, I KNOW, that in all my efforts of working with youth in the Children's Court to try to help them, there were only three individuals, or cases, whom I couldn't help. I reached a point where I did my best, but I couldn't go any further with them, so I referred them on. It still bothers me that I could have done better, but then I think that these three individuals were young people, and the parents or guardians had not been cooperative enough to help them. The ones I feel bad about are the ones that aren't here anymore. The ones that killed themselves or were committed to life in prison.

These are the ones I referred to other professionals who I thought could help them, but their parents did not step in to get them that help.

In one case, the mother didn't follow through with what I recommended. I even made appointments for both of them to go to a mental health professional. In this situation, the mother didn't follow through at the time she needed to in order for her son to get help; eventually, he killed himself. I prayed for both of them. It was tragic. I felt bad about that afterwards. There are so many things I can do and can't do. I can't predict what is going to happen in the future. We pray that the parent will do their part in helping, but that doesn't always happen. That's one of the young people that I can think of who we lost, and though it is just a memory, it feels like it just happened yesterday.

When I was asked to talk to students who were graduating from a master's program in the area of counseling at Sinte Gleska, I spoke with them about the **Wolakota** (spiritual) side of counseling. I gave them words of wisdom to help them as professionals coming into the field to help our people. To prepare themselves, I told them that our people have years and years of unresolved trauma that we are carrying. I also shared with them about how, in order to help us, they really need to ground themselves because they can really get burned out. It doesn't stop with one individual or one family because there are more in the extended family who are dealing with the same situation that you are trying to help. I recommend that our Native counselors help our people get strong spirituality, if they are going to do good work in their field. Many of our people are extra-sensitive, or emotional, and break down easily. If you are going to be a good therapist or counselor, you have to be strong spiritually to help our people.

I don't know how many churches I have been to on the Reservation with people in recovery. I go with them because there is so much gossip about them when they go to church or places of ceremony. I encourage them, and go with them, to help create the opening **Oko** (crack or opening) or **Tiopa** to **Tunkasila**. Sometimes we are scared because we feel guilty about all of the things we have done wrong when we were unhealthy; we are afraid we would not be accepted through that doorway. To have a helper with us to guide us through that doorway and hold our hand so we don't have to do it alone is very important, as the return to prayer is necessary for recovery. The next time you can go through that doorway yourself, because you know that **Tunkasila** will allow you to come through, that you will be accepted.

One of the hardest things for the human Spirit is rejection. So many times, in that unhealthy world, a mom or dad says, "You're nothing but a blankety-blank-blank, just like your mom, just like your dad or the other a-holes in your family." So, you have a reference that you are just like the a-holes in your family, and that makes you feel weak when trying to come back to the energy of **Tunkasila**.

I remind people in recovery that you are at a place of worship for yourself, your family, and the person or people you want to pray for. And you are there for God, **Tunkasila**. You are there for your belief in God, **Tunkasila** (Grandfather). In some places when I show up at a church, there are people talking about me because they think I'm lost. They must say, "He's finally admitted that our way of prayer is good and his is not." [Laughter] No, really, I'm just helping people in recovery to get going in their belief. Whatever your practice and prayer, whatever religion you are involved in, it will be a good one. Whatever that religion, you should be reverent in practicing it, not dilute it, or else you lose your connection to God, and you will look for some holy person to try to save you. I stay away from anyone who talks about a Lakota doing a Ghost Dance because it's not our belief. If you take someone away from their religion or spiritual belief, it's like cutting the kite with a string. If you cut the string, then *adios* to the kite. Believe in your practice and way of prayer, whatever that is. You are grounding your Spirit by consistency. Practice it every day. When you have consistency, you find safety and security.

For Lakota, we must start to better understand the true teachings of the sweat, the Sundance, and other ceremonies. So, there are a lot of things that people need to know about that are related to our spiritual way. Even the songs we sing, the drum, the drumstick, the vibration of the sounds all have meaning. The downbeats mean something. The 4 downbeats in our social dance represent the 4 corners of our life. You see men and women bow their heads down to the downbeats to represent thanksgiving to Mother Earth. A lot of Tribes don't understand that protocol. Why do we do that? Why do we bow our heads and lift our arms when certain songs are sung? All those teachings have meaning. It's the "Why" of what we do.

For Lakota, we have a ceremony called **Woasnikiya** or **Woapiya** (Healing of the Spirit or fixing or mending the Spirit). Very few people do this ceremony anymore, and their Spirits stay lost. Within this ceremony is the "Calling the Spirit Back." If someone's Spirit has been traumatized, they will need to go through this ceremony to get their Spirit back into their body. (The word **Wo** is in there because it's about the Spirit.) We have always believed that the Spirit gets pulled away from our body during and following trauma. Scientists have finally learned this in the study of post-traumatic stress disorders and reactions. While western medicine provides mental health counseling for the mind, the **Woapiya** (healing trauma) ceremony is like counseling for the Spirit of that trauma. That's how you heal the Spirit after trauma.

What leads up to the ***Woapiya*** is the ***Woakipa*** (Spiritual trauma) because something heavy has fallen on top of their Spirit. ***Woakipa*** would be something very bad that happened to a person, like an assault, and it's worse when inflicted by a person's own relatives or someone they love. The sensitive time for experiencing a ***Woakipa*** is from conception to 2-years old. These are the hardest ***Woakipa*** to heal, those that occur with babies.

When ***Woakipa*** happens, the body, the mind, and the soul need time to heal. ***Woakipa*** may also be the loss or death of a family, friend, pet, parent, spouse, or intimate relationship. If we take shortcuts to this healing process, we carry negative energy into the next relationship. Healing takes *time*.

In the past, a sacred rite, called "keeping and releasing of the soul" (Spirit) was practiced. For one year, or more, a hair lock of the deceased relative was kept in a rawhide pouch and placed outside the tipi on a tripod, indicating that this family is in mourning. During this time in the tipi, the deceased's place was always respected. Food was offered to the Spirit who has gone on. A little bit of each food the family prepared for that meal is placed in the location where that person normally ate to honor and show love for that relative. This is also a part of the healing and grieving. Their daily actions were practiced in a humble way. They did not practice any negative energy at this time of keeping the soul (Spirit), one of the 4 sacred rites. At the end of this rite, a releasing ceremony called "releasing the soul" (Spirit) was done. The people all respected this rite and welcomed the grieving family back into the Circle of Life; when the releasing was completed, so was their grieving. This provided an important closure.

Recognition of families in mourning is very important. Honoring of the Spirit encourages the Spirit to keep trying in whatever the learning is, despite experiencing ***Woakipa***. During this time the family is able to cry. It is a time to create discipline to acknowledge that grieving, because you are not whole at that time when you lose someone you love. If you experience trauma or violence in which you do not lose a person in your life but lose something else, like your sense of safety or your sense of worth, you still need time to heal. But in all of the experiences of **Woakipa** you have lessons that you must learn.

The Spirit is only treated through ceremony. Usually, there are misdiagnoses by mental health workers, and medical doctors often overload the human beings with pharmaceuticals that inhibit the ability for the Spirit to come back into the body. We will hear people describe someone on psychotropics as "dull" or "blunted" in their personality. Their Spirit may not even be in the body, even though they may go through the motions and be able to maintain themself physically. It also creates more addiction for many medications and comes with long-term consequences, many of which we are just now learning about.

Healing from **Woapiya** must be done with a good man from a good altar in order for good outcomes to occur. He treats the Spirit through ceremony. If the Creator wants us to continue to live, he will give us instructions to live our life through the Medicine Man, through the open **Tiopa**. We must follow these instructions if we are to continue to live.

On the other hand, if the Creator doesn't grant another day of life, some Spirits come back into this world (reincarnation) and need to go back through that learning journey again. When they lose their life, then that is the act of the Creator as part of the completion of a Blueprint.

Let's say a man named Andrew Jackson has no pity or heart for the people, or for his other relatives: He would be brought in to experience a trauma that would take his life to teach him how it feels to be on the other side of the coin. It may not be just that one time, it may have happened many times, and he keeps coming back reincarnated. That's the decision that is made by the **Inya**, the Creator. It's out of a Medicine Man's hands when it is supposed to be done that way. If he tries to bend universal law, then the Medicine Men will have to deal with or inherit the consequences too as a part of his journey and life lessons. A lot of Medicine Men won't go there, if they are smart enough, as there are lethal consequences that will happen. There are limits to what a Medicine Man would or could do.

An uncle of mine who was a Medicine Man went on a fishing trip with me, my dad, and my brother. He put a bundle in the trunk. We went out to dig for worms near this lake; he dug a separate hole from where we were digging, and then he took the bundle from the trunk and buried it. He told my dad, "I'm putting up my ***Canupa*** because people are not respecting the Sacred Pipe." Long after he passed on, a son of his who was looking for a shortcut to be a Medicine Man asked me where those pipes were buried. In this story, two universal laws were at play. One is that he was trying to bend the law of fortitude. I was tested with bending the law of wisdom. I didn't bend it. I never told him where they were buried, and they remain under the ground today.

I can only speak about this from a Lakota perspective, as I do not know what other Tribes are dealing with. However, the United States government and the men who represented that government, spread treaties of lies from the east to the west. I think these broken treaties, broken promises, and broken words impacted all of our Tribes, all over the world. The reason why our Tribal people believed that the treaties would be honored, is because it is universal law that you keep your word. You do what you say you will do. Two things came to the gathering of the signing of the treaty in April of 1868. One was the sacred ***Canupa*** (positive energy) that came from our people and allies, the other was the whiskey that was brought by the Europeans (negative energy). They passed out whiskey at the treaty signing. I ask that question to the people: Which one of these two energies was winning? Which of these two energies are our people following today?

I heard our grandparents say, ***Toksa*** Black Hills. They died with those words on their lips. ***Toksa*** Black Hills were the grandparents waiting on the United States government officials to honor their word and return, make restitution, for what was stolen. When the missionaries came and disrupted our way of life, a lot of people lost the teachings of the universal law and expected the Medicine Men to fix it. People may think that Medicine Men have a magic wand they can wave to make everything better. But that is not true.

Prior to European exposure, our Medicine Men were stronger in their healing practices. But after that exposure, we had more and more experiences in combating the exposure of missionaries, Indian agents, and genocidal attempts, and it disrupted our practices and ways of prayer. It diluted them. Names of plants and herbs, harvesting knowledge, and so much other wisdom has been lost or confused over time. Even the prayer is weaker today because of the chaos that we are living in. **Hunkasni** (physical, mental, spiritual weakness) is often what you get today.

One year at the ceremony we were trying to do something, and a Lakota elder who was highly educated in the White man's schools told us, "You guys are using too much dogma." This is relevant to the weakening of our practices that we have seen over time. We need to remove the "rational blinders" placed on our people that have been holding us back. Just because science hasn't proved something yet, doesn't mean it doesn't exist. We must believe, observe, and learn how to use the superpowers that we were all born with, that were passed down from our ancestors for us to live.

During my crazier days of following the Pow-Wow trail, I kept having returning dreams that were calling my Spirit back.

In 1976, I was in Sioux Valley, Manitoba, Canada, with a son and a wife. We were invited to a child's birthday party and feast, given by my wife's relatives.

While at the feast, an elder stood up and spoke in Dakota. He prophesied how this child is going to grow up and what the child would be as an adult. He also said a prayer, in Dakota, during his talk, and though he started crying, he continued praying. When he completed his prayer, I realized how powerful it was from the tears in my eyes and the lump in my throat.

I had an awakening then, one of Spirit. I awoke to the understanding of how our Lakota, Dakota, Nakota language is Spirit-based.

In 1983, while still on the road of alcohol and acting crazy, the Spirit dreams kept coming back. During this time, I still did not listen to ***Tunkasila*** (Grandfather, God, Higher Power). I know that what I was doing was not good, but after suffering the pain of divorce, separation from my sons, a second marriage going down in history, a head-on car wreck, near loss of my right eye, my mother's death in 1984, and finally, one long drunkenness from the second week in June, 1985, to September 12, 1985, I finally woke up when I heard a voice that said, "You're not done yet." I was in my auntie's basement in Rapid City, among empty beer bottles and cans. One of my nephews had stuck by me during my extended alcohol binge, and he was also lying down there with me. I asked, "Nephew is that you?" He said, "Yes." I said, "Where are we?" He said, "I think at auntie's in Rapid City." I asked, "How did we get here?"

Suddenly, I saw my whole life going past me and the dreams came back to me. I realized that, in my dreams, my relatives were all telling me to quit using alcohol and other medicating chemicals and to help our ***Mitakuye*** (relatives, the people).

I told my nephew, "I am going to quit drinking for good. Let's go see our cousin Leo, who is also on the wagon, and he will help us" (A.A. program).

I told my cousin Leo what my intentions were, and how I wanted to choose the most difficult road to walk on in sobriety, that of our sacred Lakota ***"Canupa Canku"*** (Sacred Holy Pipe Road). I said that after I get over the shakes, vomiting, and hangover sickness, I want to go to our Sacred Black Hills, the sacred ***"Mato Tipi"*** (Bear Butte) and make my commitment to quit using alcohol and other drugs.

The day we went up to Bear Butte, east of Sturgis, South Dakota, it was partly cloudy, and the clouds were hanging low. When Bear Butte came into our sight, the clouds covered the top part of Bear Butte. I gave tobacco to my cousin, and my nephew, and told them to start praying. When we got out of the pickup and started our climb towards the top, we got up so far and went our separate ways to pray.

I took my tobacco in my hand and found a place on top and started praying. I went as far back as I can remember, physically, mentally, spiritually, and prayed for forgiveness to those whom I had hurt. The tears started rolling down my face. I let all the hurt, pain, anger, resentment, hatred towards myself, my dad, past relationships, relatives, God, ceremonies, Spirits, all and more go. I had anger towards my dad, who had changed when he started using alcohol. I prayed for him and all others who I had anger towards, "I forgive you, please forgive me."

I do not know how long I was there on Bear Butte, crying and praying, but I realized my eyes started hurting and no more tears were coming out. It was getting late.

That day on September 15, 1985, I was reborn, **Wakini Yelo** (spiritually reborn).

On that Butte I had a vision, a spiritual contact by **Tunkasilas** (Grandfathers/Spiritual Guardians), telling me what I needed to do while I am still here on **Ina Maka** (Earth Mother). I am very grateful to the **Tunkasilas** I have met and their positive outlook on life. They have helped me and others with their presence here on **Ina Maka**. **Wopila tanka iciciya pelo** (A big thank you). Their sharing of knowledge and wisdom has helped those of us who are reaching out.

— PART 2 —

Wowakan Cekiyapi
(THE WELCOMING)

Wowa Timahupi
(INCOMING SPIRITS TO THIS WORLD)

Creating Balance for
the Mind and the Spirit

IN THE OLD DAYS, the midwife and family would go off into the woods, and it was a ceremony to give birth. No men were involved. The midwife did the welcoming. Before she cut the umbilical cord, the midwife made a commitment that she would teach the Spirit everything they needed to know about the world. (We don't call them a baby, we call them a Spirit. **Waohola** means taking care of that Spirit.) The whole camp knew which tipis had pregnant women living in them, so when they passed those tipis, they only said positive comments. They used that term, **Wowaiglusaka**, a woman who was strengthening her body to give birth. Since she was co-creating life, there was a lot of sacred energy there. During that time of pregnancy, the **Tiopa** was open.

I liked this Medicine Man who talked on KILI radio about opening the ***Tiopa***. He said that the whole community was involved in welcoming the new Spirit since there were no doors on the tipi as a sign of welcoming and love. The tipi is always open, which is a sign of generosity with an open door. The first thing that happens when we go through the doorway is that we are provided with water and food, a medicine offering of love.

Later on in my years in life, I started to understand ***Woayapi*** (how energy rubs off on us and others) by observing the negative behavior and energy of my own brother. The behaviors we make also form the energy we have. He became an alcoholic and behaved in a way that caused me not to love him anymore. A lot of those light bulbs came on for me when I started to go to school at a higher level. That is why I went to certain aunties and uncles' homes that had good loving energy, and why their food tasted good. It was because that auntie had good energy on her shoulders. It may not have been the best food in the world, but it was how she prepared it. It was all because of the auntie's good energy and the way she felt about her children—and the way she felt about me—that made her food good. The loving energy I felt from my aunt and uncle gave me more respect for them, so I would go out of my way to help them. In those days, almost everyone burned wood, so it was always a chore to chop and burn wood. We had to pump water from a pump. I did not wait to be told, I would just help them. If my aunt required any help that involved labor, I would do it. That was my way of saying thank you. She was such a good Spirit. In turn, she would go out of her way to make me feel loved. My uncle, too.

Unconditional love is a gift you get from your healthy relatives. It's the kind of love that was taught to us at an early age. I remember writing a story about my mom one time. I was a sophomore in high school, and I think it was during an English class. I can't remember the topic, but it was something about who your heroes or heroines were. When I think about my heroes, I know one of them was my mom. After I was age 12, my dad died, and my mom gave me a lot of support, even after she passed on. My mom would say, "Don't touch what is not yours." Today I call that discipline. Discipline to love and care for others. When people would tell my mom, "You have a good boy," you could see my mom's face glow. She was so proud she had a good son. Even as I grew up as an adult, I tried to do my best to make my mom's face glow. It's with pride or something. It made me try hard to finish 8th grade, 12th grade, and to receive my bachelor's degree when my mom was able to attend my graduation. She passed away before I could complete my graduate degree, but when I did, I said, "This is for you, Mom."

When she was alive, I used to buy her a bucket of Kentucky Fried Chicken and a carton of Pall Mall unfiltered cigarettes. A couple of years after she passed in 1984, I impulsively pulled into a Kentucky Fried Chicken to buy her a bucket. As I was traveling home, I got on top of the hill and saw the Red Leaf community where she is buried off in the distance, and I remembered that she was really gone. Regarding the cigarettes, she didn't inhale them, but she enjoyed them for some reason. She always had mothers, grandmas, and aunties show up at the house and they would sit and visit and smoke. Back then they had those Bull Durham roll-your-own cigarettes that demonstrated all of their patience.

Women carry that unconditional love because they care for our children. The women had respect for each other. One of the grandma's names was Ellis, and she would stop in mid-sentence and roll her own Bull Durham, and it would be quiet and no one would talk or interrupt for several minutes. Then when she was done, she would pull out her great big old strike matchstick from the box and look for the place to light it. And when she was ready, she would start talking again. No one would say anything; they would just wait. My mom would make me sit there—she wanted me to observe and learn something. Maybe it was patience and respect that you don't interrupt people, especially elders. You sit there quietly. It was so quiet I could hear the wick burning in the kerosene lamp. I could hear a fly buzzing around and the wind-up clock ticking away. Tick, tick, tick. It was that quiet.

The teaching of the young boys is that the woman is a gift from God. Today, the young men are calling women bad names and misusing them. Today, I tell young men that they need to be there at the birth of their children, so they can see life and how precious it is. Many times when you hear some man going through a re-awakening, it is when he is in jail or prison. He wants to be with his children, and he cries. He needs to experience the gift of life. That Sacred Energy. There are two doorways, one from the spiritual world and the other in the physical world. The grounding of the Spirit within the body of the baby has to be completed in both worlds.

There is a relative of mine who had a tough time getting pregnant, and when she did, she would miscarry (spontaneous abortion). When she was very young her mom and dad broke up, and her dad constantly berated her mom. She lost respect for her mom. If you do that day in and day out with your children, you can make them hate their parents. It's causing the body and the mind to get stuck in a groove of negativity toward the parent. When her dad creates an unhealthy family, he is prophesying to the daughter that as a "mom to be," these negative things are going to happen, so the message the dad sends her is, "Don't get pregnant. You're going to have to raise that baby by yourself." When a woman does get pregnant, if she is bombarded with negativity while she is pregnant, she will go through a time of doubt. When there is doubt, the mind does not prepare the body for a strong healthy womb. It builds a weak womb that will not carry the child the entire 9 months. That negativity and doubt does not allow the womb to be strong. The Spirit controls the mind and the mind controls the body.

The reason a woman may not be able to carry and birth a child often goes much deeper than the physical. If there is no sincerity, if there is doubt, or if the energy of love is not there, the whole completion will not be reached because the Spirit will go home. That will happen because the mother is closing the door, the ***Tiopa***. The sad part is sometimes the women don't know they are the cause of it, or that their negative relatives are the cause of it.

In the case of my relative trying to conceive, spiritual healing needs to happen for this to occur. She needs to find love again. She is carrying her dad's anger and doubt with her into her pregnancies. She lost 4 babies this way, and that has contributed to her being an alcoholic. What led to the breakup of her parents, was that the mother was with another man who she eventually married. Then the dad berated the new stepdad, calling him a "he-whore." Then, when the children got mad at the stepdad, they would call him a he-whore too. There would be huge family fights, further contributing to the negativity. The dad continued to tell his daughter how he was left alone and abandoned to raise her and her siblings and how much money it cost to raise a child. He further enforced the idea that she should never get pregnant until she could be sure she was with someone who would stick it out with her over the long haul.

It is critical for the parents, grandparents, and other relatives to watch what they are saying in front of a woman at the age of child-rearing. Both genders must be open to healing. No one can wave a wand and make the problems disappear. It's going to take some time for her to unwind from the ball of emotions, so she can say, "I love you Dad, I love you Mom" and be able to truly love so she will be able to conceive.

The lucky ones are those who are raised with our traditional values. I am one of the lucky ones. Lucky me! When I was growing up, I didn't realize I was that lucky. After I got to the point where I sobered up, traditional values were my resiliency. I don't throw it out there and rub it in people's faces. I am just happy that I was taught these values. I'm glad I stopped drinking, or I would have been in prison, six feet under and reincarnated again. I was thinking about doing something that would incriminate me. I was thinking about revenge. Before I did that, I found ***Tunkasila*** (God), and I let it go.

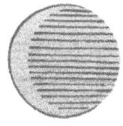

Woicaga
(Growing in a Good Spiritual Way)

Puberty Rights (W, W, W, W)

*T*HE SECOND QUARTER OF LIFE begins after the puberty rite or rite of passage; this is the second stage of ceremony, which is the welcoming. When the **Wakanyeja** reach puberty, for the female, it is their first menstrual cycle, and is a ceremony called **Isna tipi** (living alone). During this ceremony, all the elder women of the girl's family help teach this young lady how to be a woman, spouse, mother, and grandmother. These elder women protect these young girls by keeping them separate from the boys. Everything about her body-mind-Spirit is acknowledged, as a life-giver and sustainer. **Wakan ki woksape yuha mani piyelo** (They walk with that Sacred Energy).

For the male, it is when his voice starts to change. It is time for him to go on a hill and fast, **Humbleciya.** His father, uncles, grandfathers, and older brothers all help in preparing this young boy to communicate with **Tunkasila** (Grandfather/God). Vision Quest or **Humbleciya** is having **Tunkasila** remind him of his purpose, how to live his life according to the universal law and a spiritually positive code to help him walk on Mother Earth during his Circle of Life. Sometimes you are made aware if you are to be a Medicine Man, and how to prepare for this role. What the **Humbleciya** does is help you understand and bond with your Blueprint, what you are meant to do here on earth.

The elders have said that if one deviates, or does not follow these instructions of your Blueprint, there is negative suffering, imbalance, or unhappiness mentally, physically, or spiritually.

Those Medicine Men or women who have gone on to the Spirit World are going to return. How are we preparing our young and families to receive **Wakan** (spiritual good energy), as saviors, Medicine Men and women, who are healers returning to **Ina Maka** (Mother Earth) for the people?

In the movie, *The Lion King*, they teach us about the rite of passage. A child learns to talk and communicate with understanding, usually at around 4 or 5 years old. Remember in that film when the son of Mufasa left the territory and the hyenas were going to eat his kid? Mufasa showed up and saved his child. The parrot, who is like the uncle or teacher for the young ones, took the female cub back to the mother so Mufasa could talk to his son. He takes his son to a hill at night under the stars. Mufasa teaches his son about the Circle of Life and our connection to the ancestors in the stars. In our world, Mufasa is an auntie or grandma or older sister that gives those teachings for the young woman and like an uncle or grandpa for the young men. At that early age, the grandmother's energy takes over for the female and the grandfather's energy takes over for the male. It is wisdom that they are being taught to prepare them for that rite of passage. This is when a person learns to become independent. Every adult that you meet who is older than you, you should call them auntie or uncle.

The current status of a majority of our young people is that they are not walking a good road and are shortening their stay here on **Ina Maka** (Mother Earth). Many of our young people are addicted to social media, TV, video games, etc. Some need to listen to or watch TV while studying, learning, and even sleeping. Because of not learning patience and living in the fast lane, they want things now. They look for shortcuts. There are no shortcuts.

The 7th direction, which is yourself, is the most important direction. You must know yourself and understand yourself before you can know or understand the other six directions.

The second quarter of life is after the puberty rite, for both girls and boys. In this quarter you can now make life, give life. In the past, the sacred area that made life was shared only when a marriage by the **Canupa Wakan** (Sacred Pipe) made two people, as one, for life. However, today, this is very different. There have been generations of men dehumanizing women and of our third gender. This has broken our sacred connections to one another. The result of this dehumanization is trauma and chaos that disrupts the balance of healthy relationships. Alcohol and drugs further traumatize relationships.

In the past, after the puberty rite, a person was eligible to get married and raise a family. The wisdom and mentality of a 14-year-old back then is comparable to a 30- to 40-year-old today, because those early teachings and spiritual grounding were provided then. Today, people generally don't know the "why" behind church rituals or ceremonies. They don't know anything about the sacred rites. Because of this there is chaos, people living in a fantasy make-believe world of anger, hatred, and apathy. "So what if I go to jail, or prison? Mom or Dad did!"

Also, in this quarter now, many are having babies and being parents, while the majority of them have no parenting skills. This quarter is the **Wakanyeja** (sacred children) stage. If a **Wakanyeja** was abused sexually, suffered severe beatings, or had early exposure to adult situations, such as violence, they grow up faster.

Because of past negative abuse by professionals in schools, laws were created on student contact, no touching. **Wakanyeja** need hugs, nurturing, and honoring from adults. The school could do this on a weekly basis with "heart-get-togethers." For example, a drum can be brought in, the **Wakanyeja** can be lined up, and a respected school leader, and a mom or dad, can say good things to them, then everyone can hug them, wish them well. An honor song could then be sung for them while their parents watch. The drum symbolizes the heartbeat, for without the heartbeat, there is no life. The schools taking this initiative can help with producing a productive young adult. The honor of one is the honor of all.

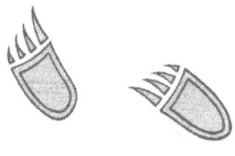

— PART 3 —

Wowakan Skan Skanpi
(HEALING/LIVING ENERGY/ACTION)

Wa Maka Skan
(MOVEMENT OF SACRED DIRT)

[Tokala calls me one day for a writing session. It is spring; I have my door open, and the birds are chirping. He shared this narrative in one sitting . . . .]

I HEAR CROW! [Excitedly] I didn't realize how happy the birds were until I went on a hill to fast for **Humbleciya** before sunrise, and it starts with one bird and then they wake each other up. It's good energy. It's like they are saying good morning to each other. It's sacred energy, it's happiness. In Creation we all have living energy called **Wa Maka Skan**, which literally means moving dirt. This refers to anything that comes from and returns to dirt, which includes four-legged, two-legged, winged ones, those who live in the ground, those who live in the water, and those who grow in the dirt including trees, flowers, plants, and grass. Today, people say **Wa Maka Skan** to refer to the Animal Nation, but really, it's about all living beings moving from the dirt.

In the spring, lightning and thunder bring that energy of love back to Mother Earth. In our Creation story, **Inyan** (Creator, Grandfather, God) wanted to be closer to the people because of the love he had for them. **Inyan** was a big rock that had blue blood. **Inyan** created earth, and since **Inyan** loved what he had created—the **Wa Maka Skan** (Animal Nation)— he wanted to be close to his creation, so he created another energy of himself called **Wakiyan Oyate** (Thunder and Lightning Beings). The thunder and lightning that returns every spring brings the energy of life. It reawakens the seeds and all the animals who sleep in the wintertime. They are awakened by the sounds and vibrations of the **Wakiyan** to Mother Earth to bring them back to life. And then, the life cycle starts over all again, **Hocoka**. These Thunder and Lightning Beings return during our spring equinox and are referred to as the **Cansasa Ipuciye** equinox, which means the red ember coming from the sacred fire to the red willow inside the pipe bowl that comes from the stars.

Cansasa Ipuciye is what we put in our pipe—it's not tobacco, it's red willow that has to be cut before the spring equinox. At that time, it is December, January, or February. If you cut it after, it's bitter; it doesn't have that good energy. A lot of our ancestors say there is a time and place to cut medicine, our herbs, when to collect our plants that help us with our health. There was a time and place for when it should be harvested. Medicine from Mother Earth comes through the root of the plant and goes up the stem and reaches the top. It spreads its energy by budding out. It releases seeds. When it does that, the energy goes back to Mother Earth and the plant goes into rest because the root will start growing again in the springtime.

I can tell by anyone's medicine—whether tea, powder, or liquid—if it has been cut too early or cut too late. If so, it has no potency. When it's cut on time, it works.

The red coal, or ember, is what gives the prayers in the pipe bowl life. With each pinch of the red willow that we put into a pipe bowl, it is a prayer. There are 7 of these prayers made, and the coal gives the pipe bowl (prayer) life. Every 7 pinches are 7 prayers to signify the 7 directions. The red coal is giving the pipe bowl life, which represents the spring energy coming to Mother Earth.

Today, some white people are selling sage and other traditional medicines. They do not always know the full teachings and often do things incorrectly in a way that causes harm. They cut medicine anytime they want, and some even pull medicine from the root, which means it will never regrow there in the future. What some White people learn from us, they take and use for their own financial gain. Some are selling back to us our own medicine that we taught them about, even selling back our language to us. When you buy traditional medicine from the market, the vendor or whoever buys it, they might be selling a weak or unhealthy plant that doesn't have potency. Even the smell of someone's sage or sweetgrass—I can tell when it is weak. With sage, if people collect it at the appropriate time, it's pungent. If you are downwind, you can smell its potency. Out of respect, you don't pull the plant out of the ground. That way, it can regrow again. However, if the cure is in the root, then you only take what is needed.

The grandmas are the ones who sing to the plant and harvest these plants because of their sacred energy. In the 1960s, grandmas were saying that global warming was impacting our traditional medicines so that they were not reaching full potency to heal. These challenges continue today as we must go farther and farther to find the medicines we need for our healing ceremonies. When the weather turns hot then quickly cold, the plants do not know what to do. When there is flooding and drought, the plants have little chance to survive.

I know a Medicine Man who has that awareness of a plant that he cuts to help people with cancer. That has to be done, too, at the appropriate time. If it's not cut at the appropriate time, it loses its potency. The chosen people who are supposed to be doing these things have a dream, through the dream **Tunkasila** is telling them to cut it at the appropriate time. **Tunkasila** will give you a picture of the plant, how it looks. When you go look for that plant, it will talk to you. You'll know.

We have Medicine Men who have that power, the herbal people. There are many different types of medicine people. Some work with Spirits, some work with eagles and different types of animals. Usually when you receive some type of power from the Creator you nurture it, you take care of it, you don't abuse it. When you abuse it, you lose it. If we start doing something bad to others, we will lose the power we were given. People are aware that they have the gift, but they don't use it in a good way. They should fully understand and educate themselves on that gift, so they can be in balance with it. If you neglect a gift, it doesn't help you or your relatives. There are protocols that we must follow, and we have to respect our gifts. There are no shortcuts.

A lot of our Medicine Men, long ago, before exposure to Europeans, had that special way of life. They did things in the daytime. They openly showed their powers in the daytime. Then when Europeans came, and they pushed their European religions on our people, we moved ceremonies and practices to nighttime. Our ceremonies and practices went underground. When they went underground that meant that other energy, bad energy, began to infiltrate it. Some spiritual people were unaware that dark energy can come in at night. Dark energy and light energy have the same power, but dark energy can lead you to evil things when it is too late. Some don't realize they are using dark energy until then.

Greed is one of the examples of the dark energy that has come to our people. People started becoming something they are not. They wanted money or wealth. When I was 17 or 18, I saw this eagle feather elevate from my uncle's altar in the daytime when he was praying. It went up in the air and made a few circles and then gently landed back on the altar again. That's what made me a believer. I became reborn. I was like, "Wow!" I still thought it might have been a fishing string controlling it, but there was no string. I thought that was awesome. Then I became reborn into our belief and had curiosity about that belief. When I was seeing things with my own eyes, it made me a believer. I saw how medicine people lost their power by going to the dark side. They may think they have it, the good energy, but it may not be a good energy helping them. They get deeper and deeper into that dark side without always knowing it.

There are tricks a human being can play on another human being under the cover of darkness without anyone seeing the tricks being played on them. That encouraged a lot of the fake medicine people. It wasn't just one; it became many fake medicine people shadowed by the darkness of night. When our spiritual ways went underground, that's when fake medicine people started popping up too. Today I respect only three altars.

Good prayer should be brought back to light, to practice in the daytime. We won't be sent to an insane asylum anymore by practicing our way of prayer during the daytime. It's also an important step for decolonization to bring our ways back out into the light. That will help us weed out the bad or the fake. In the old days, medicine people would show the people what their power was in the light, and that's why people would come to them for help. In return people would give them things for what they received, for their **Wopila** for Thanksgiving and being thankful for what the healer had done to help them. In the past, a person gave meat, food, blankets, tools, or other things they had to give. Today, a person usually gives cash to pay for gas and the healer's helpers (singers, drummers, wood collectors, etc.) and to contribute something to the Thanksgiving feast after. I need a singer, some of those songs are long and you can't always sing and heal at the same time. When a Medicine Man is interpreting the invisible to the physical for the person who is asking for prayer, his energy needs to be there and focused on the person he's helping. The interpreter's helpers are a vital part of the ceremony in order not to exhaust the Medicine Man or Woman so they may focus their energy on the healing. The helpers can go into the Sweat Lodge, chop the wood, build the fire, gather the rocks, help cover the lodge, put stones in the lodge, and perform many other helping tasks. The interpreter then shares whatever he or she received as Thanksgiving gifts with the helpers, so they are also cared for. Today, that is still the protocol.

For Lakota, a sweat occurs before the healing. Anyone who is going to partake in the **Lowanpi** (ceremony involving singing prayer songs for healing) or **Yuwipi** (spiritual person is tied up or bundled in the ceremony until the Spirit unties them as a part of the healing for the person) must go through sweat by protocol. Participants or supporters who are able to go into the lodge are asked to also come into the sweat. Usually, a Medicine Man would not only do one healing, but would invite three or four other individuals who needed healing to come and take part at that time. That way the families share feeding the people with food, so it's not just one family who has to put on the feast after the ceremony. It's like group therapy. We also get strength from one another when we go through a healing process together. We create a bond with individuals who practice our way of prayer by coming to the same altar of that Medicine Man, and we build that respect and love for each other. It is love when you pray for somebody, which is helpful in the healing process.

A person coming for healing also has supporters, who are often the family of that individual and will come and help support the prayer. One person might have two or more supporters. Some individuals come with large families, so it could be as many as fifty. When that happens, not everyone can fit in the Sweat Lodge, so they remain in prayer outside the lodge for support. It's just standard that we do these protocols.

The word *love* is really important. It is a critical term here. It begins at the beginning of life. **Tunkasila** loves life to create life. It comes from love, the creation of life, Mother Earth, and all of the **Wamaka Skan Oyate** (Animal Nation). We come from that family of love.

I was told that when Europeans came from the East Coast, there were hardly any flat lands. There were trees and all different types of herbs everywhere. Medicine was abundant.

When my daughter was born, we learned through ceremony that her guardians were a blue bird and a yellow bird. The blue bird and yellow bird always showed up during her years of growth at our home. Daily, they would be sitting on the fence post or the highline wire to let us know that they were there. So, my daughter would come running into the house excitedly saying, "Dad, they're out there." She was really happy her guardians were out there. I thank **Tunkasila** for sending those guardians to help her.

When we moved into the house we live in, it's about a mile out in the country. We have a lot of trees, pine and cedar. All these wild turkeys come around and eat in our front yard. I throw scraps out there. I feel like I'm a farmer with all of these wild turkeys running around our house. My son named one of those turkeys one time. It was an albino turkey, and my son had named it Edgar. When it's turkey season, hunters come and kill the turkeys. My son prays for the turkeys, too. During turkey season, he would say, "Fly away, Fly Away." They would come around looking for food and they would come close to him. That's a good thing about raising kids out away from the city. The city was too noisy and had a lot of unhealthy behavior, negative influences.

A lot of us have energies that we are unaware of, that we are born with. We need to come to people who are knowledgeable about it to help us reconnect with those energies. Once you start to reconnect with the energy, you can create the balance and harmony with it. You can keep it a secret. You don't have to go around the world saying I am this way and I am that way. It's actually more respectful if you don't. In the same way, I respect what was given to me too. I would rather be low profile than telling the world, but here I am now writing this book. Geez! [Laughter] I'm still not going to put a sign on my door saying I do this, and I do that. I don't do that because I respect it. I respect these gifts that were given to us. If someone gives you something, you are supposed to take care of it. Be in harmony with it and do good things with it, not bad things. The same goes for the gifts we are given: physical gifts like children and the ability to see, hear, and walk; spiritual gifts such as the ability to heal, prophesize the future, or connect with the past (ancestors). When we have respect for these gifts, it will help us know ourselves and our family.

Back in 1986, I went up to Bear Butte to fast for 4 days and 4 nights. The helpers there with me brought me down because there was a storm coming so they couldn't finish the **Humblecha**. Instead of having the traditional meal, we had **Wasna** (dried buffalo meat and dried chokecherries) and the sacred pipe that you smoke after the sweat. Inside the sweat you share your dreams, and the Medicine Man is there to interpret your dreams. These dreams reconnect you to your Blueprint of what you need to do to make yourself better or to get better with anything you are dealing with. This process is to help you gain clarity and understanding, and to get better.

Let's say your life is living in a dark world and to get more enlightenment you need to go through fasting and prayer. After you go through fasting and prayer, you'll see your Blueprint and, if you follow it, good things will happen. If you don't, you will go back to being out of balance. While we are in the sweat, we drink water that we didn't have on the hill while we were fasting. Outside we share **Wasna** and chokecherry juice. Then they feed us at the camp with the soup of the day. Deer soup, buffalo soup, wild game soup, but not Campbell's Soup [Laughter]. There is something about the energy of wild game that you don't get from the processed meat you buy in the stores. It's a nutrition that connects to our Spirit, our DNA, and it is how we have survived all of these years.

So, the storm was coming and my helpers said we were going to go down to a local restaurant in Sturgis, and we would have our meal down there. At the restaurant, they lined three tables together and they put me on one side. Around the table were my helpers and those who supported me through their presence and prayers as I fasted on the hill. While I was sitting there, the waitresses came in and gave us menus and water, but my Spirit was still up there on that hill. People were discussing salads and salad dressing.

There were two people who came in, and they looked like bikers. I looked up, and the White woman and I locked eyes, and we knew each other already. She came walking toward me, and I looked down. I could feel her presence coming. As I was looking down, I wasn't reading the menus, and I could feel her presence next to me. She said in a very gentle voice, "Sir, I notice something about you," and she asked if she could touch my shoulder. I looked at her eyes and she had a really good energy coming from her. She said her name and told me she was a psychic who would be doing a presentation at Black Hills State College, which is now a university. So, I nodded my head that she could touch me. She said that from where she was standing over there, she could see me glowing. And I was!

It seemed like I could hear people's thoughts and so many voices. When you are in sync with **Tunkasila** (Grandfather), you are not scared. It's a power or an energy surge that you bond with. That's when I started to really understand my spiritual side more. I always tell that story about the psychic who touched me. Before that moment when she said that to me, I knew there was a feeling I grew up with about people with different energy that I couldn't really understand when I was young. I did know, however, that I could sense that nurturing energy; I could feel people's energy. Some have brighter light, and some have dimmer light and need help.

When I became spiritually aware of the gifts I was given, I was pulling away trying to jump off the web. I wanted to bail out because I was scared of the spiritual gift. Now, I don't think I'm completely off the web. I'm still on the edge of it. I can still tune into that spiritual gift when I want, but I have more control now. Maybe I need to go back to the center of the web to get more of that energy before I am too old. I always feel that I want my children to be pretty well on their own before I go back there. There is this energy that has life and death in it. And we don't play around with it. If we mess up, then who will pay the price? If we mess up, **Tunkasila** will figure out a way to teach us. That's the sacrifice, and sometimes it hurts. That's why I respect the spiritual gifts we are given. I don't have animosity about spiritual gifts, I just respect their power.

I'm involved with our Sundance people, those who pray with the pipe today. I see a lot of good things coming out for them, too. That's my goal—to have sober alcohol- and drug-free leaders who really do care for the people rather than the money or material things that have served as a way to distract us from our healing. I see the change happening, but it's not happening fast. It's not supposed to happen fast anyway. But it's there. I can see the change in people. People don't want to be lied to anymore.

Wacante Ognaka
(Generosity)

*I*N THE PAST, THERE WERE SONGS that said, "Give as much as you can, for whatever you give you will always get back." It's a song that is sung after a giveaway. A giveaway is something done to demonstrate your generosity for special purposes. A giveaway could be honoring a relative's achievements or adoption to replace a lost loved one; it could be for any reason, happy or sad. The family who hosts the giveaway is expressing their love. There is no limit to giving. The more they gave the more they expressed love.

Generosity is a universal law, and breaking that law would be done by a person who doesn't fully give whatever they can. They only give a little. If you are not raised in a pitiful way, you don't know what it means to be pitiful. To not have pity affects love; it creates a fractionated love. Today, the families who are well off are the first ones running to the dollar store and are giving away dollar store gifts. From the outside looking in, it shows the expression of the family not really caring about themselves. If what you give comes back to you and you are giving out dollar gifts, what does that say about how you see yourself? That mindset also reflects in your children and grandchildren, and how well they do in school, how productive they are as adults, is based on that simple act of generosity. It sets a template for your children. From that point on, the generations that come will always be stingy for families who break this universal law.

I remember one time when my mom honored my niece who graduated from college. She gave her a well-deserved grandma's name. She received the name of one of our grandmas. My mom saved for an entire year, and she had relatives make Star Quilts and beaded moccasins for her. It was an entire day event that also involved a pow-wow. Dancers and singers were invited to celebrate my niece's graduation. We men in the family helped prepare an entire cow to feed everyone, and my brother claims to be the accomplished chef, so he cooked for us. The event started in the afternoon, and when it came time for the giveaway, my mom demonstrated unconditional love. A woman who talked bad about my mom and gossiped showed up. When my aunt saw this woman, she made a face like when you taste something bad and whispered something to my mom. That's how I knew the woman was not in favor within my family. My mother told the announcer to call her up. When the announcer called her up, my mother selected the most beautiful Star Quilt for that woman and draped it over her shoulders. My mom was smiling as she did that and gave her a hug and kiss on the cheek. The woman began to cry. The act of generosity is powerful and can show unconditional love. Healing occurred through generosity. You can help someone heal by showing that unconditional love.

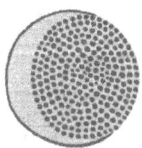

Woakipa
(Spiritual Trauma) of Indoctrination

The community where I was raised was small. In 1962, we had nine Christian churches competing for us, fighting over the souls of fewer than 100 Lakota people. That's when I was 9 years old and had first moved. The first two churches that came to my community were Episcopal on the north side and Catholic on the south side. My grandfather told my father that we were forced to be baptized.

Interestingly, I recently applied for a passport as we work to connect spiritual leaders across the Americas, and they wouldn't accept my delayed birth certificate as evidence that I was from this country, since I was born on Tribal lands in a chicken coop. Instead, they told me I could submit a baptismal certificate as the only religious documentation of three potential sets of documents on the list that they would accept as a form of proof. One group of documents included school records, which I already had sent to the passport office. I was 6 or 7 when I started school, after the police told my family that I had to go. But the passport office required documents showing schooling at the age of 5 or younger, so they didn't accept what I sent them. The second set of documents was Hospital records, which I didn't have, because I was born with

Mitakuye Oyasin, the chickens [Laughter]. I tried to call Pine Ridge, a Father somebody there, to get my baptismal certificate. Then I called Rosebud Episcopal Priest, a woman who goes by Mother something, and she told me to call a Father somebody at Pine Ridge to get my certificate. She told me it might be hard to get because the passport people want an original, and they have to get into the archives and see if it's there. I thought this was supposed to be the land of the free, yet here we are, still being controlled. I am a leftover Prisoner of War.

In the Homestead Act of 1862, the government gave settlers permission to shoot us if we left the Reservation. If a White man killed an Indian, a White man would not be punished. The reverse situation would result in an Indian being thoroughly prosecuted or even killed. Today, I still feel like I'm a Prisoner of War. There is still no justice. If baptismal papers are the only religious documentation that can let a person travel out of this country, what does that mean for all the other religions? Where is the freedom?

When my grandpa was a child, if you wouldn't choose a church, the BIA agent would flip a coin and choose it for you. If you did not get baptized, you were not a human being, according to the self-proclaimed superior race. Growing up, I saw all of these black and white photos of our Native people wearing huge crosses around their neck to tell the Christian world they were getting saved. What the Christians didn't understand is that we didn't need to be saved, we were already the superior beings because we treated human life as sacred and took care of that life. In those days, if they caught you practicing Sweat Lodge or practicing your Lakota way of prayer, then they called you insane and sent you off to an insane asylum called Hiawatha in Canton, South Dakota. They kept you there, even when you were a healthy person.

Recently I visited Hiawatha. I was asked to do a prayer for them over there. It is horrible what happened! Beyond horrible. The Indian agents and the Christians got rid of our medicine people who were normal, healthy Native people who did not want to give up their way of prayer. They did not want to get baptized. They were chained . . . well, you can just read about it. Google Hiawatha. They sent an Indian Agent from Washington, D.C., to check on why there were so many Native people still there. The agent found that most of them were healthy, so the government released them. The only reason they kept them there, was that the Christian leaders told Indian Agents that they were resistant to being "civilized," and that they had psychosis because they were speaking to their Spirit relatives. How civilized is that? How superior is that?

I saw a movie about Jesus and why they crucified him. That reminds me of our religion. We Lakota people are Jesus Christ and we were crucified, and are still being crucified. We are the saviors of the world and yet they continue to crucify us. Our knowledge about living in balance and harmony with the earth is going to save our colonizers one day. Yet they continue to crucify us.

For Indigenous people here on Turtle Island, much of our way of prayer and ceremony went underground for over 400 years. For the Lakota, our practices didn't come up in public again until 1972, when we could finally openly Sundance and have Sweat Lodges. The American Indian Religious Freedom Act wasn't passed until 1978, 486 years after Columbus was lost and landed on our shores. The U.S. Constitution was written and signed in 1787. In 1791, an amendment was made, and Religious Freedom was adopted into the Bill of Rights. The First Amendment guarantees freedom of religion, expression, assembly, and the right to petition. It forbids Congress from promoting one religion over others and restricting an individual's religious practices. It also guarantees freedom of expression by prohibiting Congress to restrict the press or the rights of individuals to speak freely. It guarantees the rights of citizens to assemble peacefully and to petition the government.

My how the self-proclaimed superior race violates their own laws when it comes to Indigenous peoples. Why is that?

To answer this question, you have to look back further for what Columbus and his cronies brought with them in terms of "intent."

In the 1400s, prior to Western expansion, the Pope of the Catholic Church wrote the Papal Bulls that gave European explorers the guidance they needed to massacre Indigenous peoples.

> *"That in our times, especially the Catholic faith and the Christian religion be exalted and be everywhere increased and spread, that the health of souls be cared for, and that barbarous nations be overthrown and brought to the faith itself."* The Papal Bulls were issued nine times with this message.

So, when Columbus and other Europeans landed here, they already had instructions to overthrow the Indigenous people and turn them to the Catholic and Christian faith.

When the Bill of Rights speaks of religious freedom, it is interpreted to exclude Indigenous peoples because we were not seen as human until we were baptized and converted to that way of greedy thinking.

So, it seems that when the Bill of Rights Amendment was adopted, the signers really only intended religious freedom for themselves.

My mom's Christian faith intensified in the 1950s. I remember going to church convocations. One time, the church members got together and saved money to hire my dad's White leaser's semi livestock trailer. He cleaned it out, and they hired my dad to take our community to Greenwood, South Dakota, along the Missouri River to the Episcopal convocation. I remember the gravel road and the semi-truck rolling down the road to the river. We were all riding in the back as if we were cattle and all the women and men were singing church songs in Lakota and Dakota. As we passed by farms, there were farmers looking at this semi-truck and hearing all of these cows singing Lakota. [Laughter.] We put all of our tipis in there too. It was our way of life to bring our homes with us.

The ones who lived along the Missouri River were first exposed to European religion. That was the Isanti (Santee). A lot of the first Tribal ministers were Santee. We got confirmed through confirmation classes when we were 11 or 12. After we got confirmed, we would receive a cross. And once we got the cross, it allowed us to receive communion, which was the taking of wine and bread, representing the blood and body of Christ. I wondered what was worse to White people, eating the blood and body of Christ or eating dog.

As a part of my Christian experiences, my mom volunteered me to be an acolyte (altar boy), who is a person who helps serve communion in the Episcopal Church. The priest wears a black robe with white on top, the acolyte wears a red robe with white on top. I and other acolytes helped mix the communion wine with water, and the priest directed me to pour the wine into the chalice. He also told me how much water and how much wine to pour for the communion. We had to cover 7 churches on a Sunday. When we first started, the priest would ask me to put more water in and less wine. Whatever the congregation didn't consume, what was left of the bread and the wine, then the priest and I, we ate and drank it up. So, by the time we hit the 7th church we were pretty happy! This was my first introduction to alcohol.

At every church we went to, there were still traditional Lakota people who fed us. So, we would always have **wateca** (leftover food) to take home, and the Lakota people kept giving it to us in boxes. We would come back with a lot of fry bread. It seems like they all served the same stuff on Sunday. Potato salad, pork and beans, sandwiches, a lot of fried chicken, cakes, and pies. So, when I came home, I would have two or three boxes, and all my brothers and sisters would run to help me because they knew there were cakes or pies. Of course, I was buzzed up, too. When we went to the last church for the day, the priest's car would be zig-zagging, and the priest would be telling stories, and then he would laugh and swerve. Of course, those were gravel road days too, which made it dangerous.

Then my mom put me in a church school for boys so I could become an Episcopal priest, but after all the Christian teaching, I graduated high school at age 18 and gave up being a Christian. I started to look around for myself. But I didn't really find myself until 1985, when I was 32. So, everything that I know and understand today did not come to me overnight. A lot of my teachings, my spiritual teachings, came from my dad, my uncles, and my grandpas who were all Medicine Men. They were spiritual leaders and taught me how to say and do things in the appropriate way with proper protocols. They were strict teachers who would teach in our language. Today, it is an honor for people to understand holistic health. They need to be taught traditionally, too, so they can find the balance they are looking for.

I like what Sitting Bull said, **Taku Waste Iyeyab Hena Yuha Mani Po Waste Sni Ki Ayustan Po**, "Take the good and leave the bad."

In 1971, I went to Ohio. I stayed out there in a Boy Scout camp for three months, and when I was out there, I went to church with one of the camp pastors. That's the first time I went to a different church. I think they were Baptist. In their way they don't use wine, they use Welch's grape juice and a large loaf of bread that is not sliced and placed on a wooden platter. They pour a small paper cup of grape juice for each person who will be receiving communion and have them tear off a piece of the bread. After you say the prayer, you eat the bread and drink the juice.

I think there was an era where our people called the sacraments **Mni Wakan** (Holy or Sacred Water). That's what they called the wine that represented Jesus's blood. I think that helped increase alcoholism even more because some of our people thought it was sacred to drink wine. If you were confirmed in the church, then that's what you had on Sunday: You had flatbread and you washed it down with wine. In a way, taking communion made our people think it was okay to drink wine. I think mentally they were covering up all the horrible things that had just happened. Whether it is beer, wine, vodka, or whatever, I call it **Mni Sica**, or bad water, to let the community know that it wasn't good. In studying history, England, France, and other places had prohibition at some time because the alcohol use got so bad. So, they knew when it came up the river in the whiskey barrels what it would do to our people. That realm of genocide was preplanned. It was premeditated. There are pictures from the Fort Laramie Treaty signing. In these photos United States representatives were sitting among our Lakota chiefs. Our chiefs were sharing the sacred pipe (a pipe that still exists) to invite the Creator to witness the treaty signing. The Europeans were passing around a brown jug, and under the picture it reads, "Treaty gifts." These jugs had corks in them and that's what they brought the whiskey, a bad medicine, to our people in.

They sent us kids to Sunday school the same time adults went upstairs to study. The first time I went to a convocation, I didn't know how to speak English, so I ran away. I ran under a car and hung on to the shaft under the car and the Sunday school teachers tried to pull me out. They pulled my shoes off, my socks off, they pulled my pants and stretched my suspenders off until they almost depantsed me. Then they went and got my mom, and I heard her calling. She gave me a gentle scolding in Lakota, because we don't have cuss words in our language. She told me to go back and learn what they were trying to teach me, so I went back to the church, picking up my clothes and putting them on as I walked.

So, I have a lot of experience with Christianity. I also went to boarding school where I read the New Testament, but I could not connect with it because it was not what happened to us. What I understand is our way of prayer and our way of ceremonies. So I can't understand what happened over there in Europe. It doesn't have any reality for me here.

Years later, two of my friends and I got snowed in at a motel in Wisconsin so we couldn't go anywhere. It snowed three, four, or five days in the woodlands. There was nothing in that motel room, and we kept watching TV. In the closet, we found one of those Bible trivia games, and we played it. That was when I was going through a bad divorce, and I was hanging out with some pretty rugged characters because we all worked in the same place. Anyway, I kept winning. They said, "Geez you're like a devil, and you keep winning." [Laughter] "Where did you learn all that?" So much so, that they didn't want to play with me anymore because I always won.

I think I'm a better or more whole person today than I was as a practicing Christian. I always tell that to people who ask questions about my spirituality. When I was a Christian, I wasn't the whole pie, there were pieces missing. I wasn't happy. Not until I started to know who I am and where I came from, and I grounded myself in our ceremonies to know what grandma and grandpa went through, did I really start to become happy. When I put myself on the hill to pray, I cried many tears thinking about what my grandmas and grandpas went through, and it helped me let go of that Christian teaching. Hanging on to the things that hurt our people is really heavy to carry every day. You'll not be a happy camper if you carry that every day of your life. To understand what our people went through, to understand the past, to live with the present, and to help prepare yourself and your family for the future—that's the way I look at life now.

My dad named me after our White land leaser. He was the White man who leased our Indian land for grazing his cattle. My dad liked what our leaser did to help us out in the country so, out of respect, the English name he gave me for the U.S. Census was after our leaser.

For myself, I wanted to change my name, so it is now my Lakota name. I achieved this through our Tribal court system. It's a long name that was given to me, **Tokala Hocoka Waokiya Ob Mani** (warrior who helps the living energy in the Circle of Life). That came from when I started a walk called *Journey to Healing* with support from the Robert Wood Johnson Foundation when I was working with some of our communities in healing our families. So, my family gave me that name and put an eagle feather on my head. That was my third honoring as a Tokala. The first honoring was at the Big Foot Memorial Ride, and the second honoring was when I earned my second master's degree, Management as a Lakota Warrior, at the Oglala Lakota College.

Sometimes, I bump heads with people who really don't go as far back in history as I do. They say **Tokala** means veteran, and I say no, it means One Who Spreads Blue Energy to the World. That's what a **Tokala** man does. That's what our men did many years ago. That is a respected name for our men. The one who goes out and spreads blue energy. Blue means good in a spiritual way.

Once the Europeans came, then we started dealing with war. A long time ago, the Indigenous Nations settled disputes through games. Each Nation, like Oneida, Lakota, Sac, Fox, and others, settled disputes over games. That's why many Tribes still have those games today such as lacrosse (stick ball), shinny games, spear throwing, archery, and others. There was no war. We didn't fight and kill one another because there was a respect for life.

In Ohio, there is a huge earth mound. It is big enough to hold four football fields. All around it is a huge wall in a perfectly round circle, and it has a door opening toward the East. I'd like to take our youth out to see that because there are artifacts, like sharp rocks that are only found in two places, the Black Hills and Arizona. How did they end up in Ohio? The most obvious idea is that we all got along. We befriended each other as we followed the buffalo. That's how the rocks got there.

I think about how we don't have angry words or cuss words in Lakota. All that stuff was taught to us by the Europeans. What they did to us, we did back to them, in the act of war to defend our people and what we had left. After the hangings of the 38+2, we saw what they did to Little Crow, and how they dragged his corpse up and down the streets of Mankato (Blue Earth). However, even in the act of war, Lakota people had limits. We did not do to Custer what the Europeans did to Little Crow and Braveheart: They tied Braveheart's legs and arms to horses and tore him apart in front of the people; they buried those parts separately. The Europeans wanted to teach us that, even in the Spirit World, our Lakota people would not be whole. He's already dead, right? You didn't have to do that! Who is the savage? Who is the heathen?

That is what happened in Mankato. This wasn't the first, and it went on and on.

During these acts of war, they beheaded Indigenous people and put them along the road in 6-mile increments in all directions to scare off other Indigenous peoples in colonial towns. The worst thing that Tribal people did to Custer was done by the Northern Cheyenne women. They spoke to Custer's Spirit and told him that, because he didn't listen, they would poke holes in his ear so he could listen in the Spirit World. That is mild *savage* behavior when compared to ripping people apart alive, beheading our people, and dragging corpses down the streets. Or even keeping their heads in the center of the town for an entire month.

Tiole
(Loss of Home)

Homeless

WE FOLLOW THE STAR MAP to locate different places on Turtle Island based on the seasons. During the fall season, we are doing Sundance in the Plains area. In the wintertime, we are in the Black Hills. In the springtime, we are all around Bear Butte, fasting and praying. In the summertime, we are back in the Plains again following the buffalo. That was our home, following the star map.

I went through the script of being a Christian. I was acting. Part of the pie was missing for me. Christianity didn't fill me. I kept my **Wolakota Hocoka** intact. After I went to college, I hung up my Christianity. That was it. That was the end!

Around that same time, I started having out-of-body experiences. It would happen when I would wake up, and I would be out of my body all day. This went on for six years. I had to get used to seeing this little boy, me, when I left my body. I saw a TV commercial about a little boy with a big backpack on his first day of school. The bag must have been as big as he was. It was some kind of insurance commercial. In the commercial, the mother walks him outside, and the bus driver is beckoning him to get on the bus. He turns around and runs back to his mom to give her a big hug and then jumps on the bus. It chokes me. I have a lump in my throat because of the love of life. What I was experiencing I don't know. I love life so much, and I thought I would never come back to my body. I had to learn to live with it. To be at peace with it. That's when I started to do some exploring, and I started to go farther and farther away from my body. But I could come back just as quickly. That is how I found out how fast Spirit travel was. I got more confident in going farther and farther away from my body. The emotions or energy that the Spirit feels. Someone would say, "Tokala, Tokala," and I would be spacing out. But I could come back to my body when someone called me. I was scared to tell them what was going on with me. What was wrong with me? At that time, I was neither aware nor in tune with my Blueprint. Once I started finding the Center of my **Hocoka** (Circle of Life), I came back into my body.

Some years later, I met Dr. Dan Foster. We talked about this experience. That's when he opened up the knowledge that I was going through heavy stages of depression. Extreme stages. This is the same way a Spirit can leave the body inside the womb when it wants to go home. When the love of a mother is not anchoring that Spirit coming into this world. The same thing can happen when you are depressed. What I was experiencing was the trauma drama of my dad, and the anger I felt. Our home out in the country where I grew up was sold for alcohol. I remember that as a sad time, when my mom and I were kicked out of my sister's house after my father passed away, leaving us homeless. We were walking through the snow in the wintertime, crying. It's still strong in my brain, in my memory. We walked to one of my auntie's houses, and we stayed there a few days. We were homeless.

After all of this, I was put in a boarding school. Of all the near-death experiences I had, I always felt that something good was taking care of me, watching over me and bringing me home safe. There was something in me that felt like a good energy. With all that I have been through, I was only sent to jail for one night. [Chuckles] Unfortunately, there was a blizzard and one night in jail turned into 7, so I learned my lesson.

During one of the holidays when we were homeless, we stayed with one of my relatives. Many of my relatives were exposed to the boarding school mentality. I must have been touching some sensitive areas that my relatives didn't want to talk about, so when my mother advocated for me, they kicked us out. This was a critical time in my life when I saw my nieces and nephews get beaten by their parents. They beat their children so bad some would stutter.

In my return to spirituality when I pray for my people, I pray a special prayer for all who experienced trauma in missionary and government boarding schools.

In all my out-of-body experience and all that depression I was feeling, in a way, I think my Spirit wanted to go home, where we come from.

Winkte Nagi Nunpa
(Two Spirit)

Understanding the Third Gender

*D*URING THE TIME before the Europeans' arrival, Lakota had a name for two-Spirit males. They were called **Winkte**, which means Kills the Woman Spirit, because they can do everything a woman can but give birth. This name was used for a male that had female attributes. **Winkte** were respected and were a part of our **Hocoka**, and they played a role that was connected to spirituality, because they had a gift. I think they may have been like See-ers, those who can see what would happen, because I was told that Crazy Horse usually took one or two **Winkte** with him to assess a cavalry's camp. When the European religions came to our people, the **Winkte** went underground too, just like our religion. Just like our religion, they were still active but not in public view. Those Lakota who began to believe and practice those European religions further promoted prejudice of the **Winkte**.

It took me a little time to be in harmony with the third gender, the two-Spirit that is returning. But after learning more information and having more exposure to current trends and trying to bond with this new (returning) gender, this third gender, today I can see how our future generations will be some day. I see how we will still carry the energy of good health and learning how to get along with each other no matter the genders we express. It's the balance and harmony of our people.

We, as elders, need to create a **Tiopa**, a doorway for the two-Spirit people to be a part of our **Hocoka** again, to be included in our circle. There is a scientific word for someone who has male and female energies in one body. The word is *Androgynous*. The word doesn't mean they are sexually both, but that females will have male attributes and males will have female attributes until you may not be able to tell the difference anymore. There is a prophecy about the world having more androgynous people as we are building up to the 4th cleansing.

Woakipa Sica
(Bad Trauma to the Spirit)

Energy of Anger

I don't want to get mad at anyone because we, as human beings, have power. If you get mad at someone you could hurt them without even touching them. A female relative of mine carried with her the negative energy of anger. She projected that anger into the world and is surrounded by people who mirror the same anger. She already knew what was wrong with her. She had a heart valve problem and diabetes. The conditions she had affected her employment and completion of goals. It also impacted her personal life.

I have come to a point now where I only give suggestions to help relatives like her, because some relatives are too aggressive, and they will tell me off. Tell me to get out of their business. So, I only give suggestions to make them better with what time we have left here on Mother Earth. To make the best of what we can do here. There are a lot of relatives who are living this way. They are hanging on to life by a thread. If they do not follow proper medication, fatal things can happen, like strokes. Today, in our life there are so many things that are critical, so many crises in our homes and communities, including grandmas trying to raise many grandchildren and put a safe roof over their heads. It's hard for these elders to leave home for more than a couple of hours because they may have many relatives living in the home who do not respect it or take care of it, and continue addictive lifestyles. You have to constantly check your home to make sure it is okay, that no one is stealing from you or burning your house down.

Anyway, this relative went through many trials and tribulations. She went through broken marriages and relationships from her past. She lost children. Even her current relationship was heartbreaking. She was living with some guy who was not being authentic with her. She asked me to bless their relationship without being totally aware of what was going on behind her back. He was already messing around on her with another woman. I met him and could tell what kind of person he was right off the bat. There was a point where I had more pity for her. She was going to quit working and enjoy her family. She was supposed to go through heart surgery, but she kept postponing it because her chances of recovery were slim. She is just one of many relatives who have health problems related to negative energy. Their **Hocoka** (Circle of Life) is daily negative energy. They wake up to it. It consumes them. They go to bed with it. It makes them sick.

A friend of mine had the same thing happen. He was drinking. He was unaware of the symptoms of diabetes. He continued to overload on sugar every time he drank. One day he collapsed. That's when he learned that his heart valves were sticking and that he needed to get them replaced. They connected his heart to a battery that opens and closes the valves to the heart. He did stop drinking but never stopped his dry drunk behavior of anger, which affected his health and exacerbated other health problems. He finally died. After he died, that thing was still going, that battery, opening and closing the valves to his heart.

The way I see it, people with diabetes, their blood becomes sticky from too much sugar. Even if they might be taking insulin. My relative was like that. Did I tell that story? One of my relatives went to a Catholic missionary school. They had a big orchard and some of the kids would go and play there. My relative is a month younger than me. We were playing in the orchard with a friend. My female relative and her female cousin each had two white bakery bags. We told them to come sit in the circle. They had bags full of sweet rolls and donuts. She gave us food, and we ate it all. Then she said, "Do you want some more?" We said yes because we had just indulged in all that sugary stuff. We were all young then.

She and the girl cousin went to the bakery at the mission school to get more. I followed them to the missionary school where the bakery was connected to the mission. That's where all the Catholics stay, the priests and the Jesuits. As I was following them, they turned around before the bakery door and said, "You can't come with us. They won't give us rolls if you come. You have to stay over there in the parking lot and wait for us." So I did. A while later, they came running downstairs and they were both holding two white bakery bags, and they were happy. The bags were, again, full of sugary snacks. They yelled for me to come on. We went back to the orchard and feasted again.

Later in life, this relative began to drink heavily, got diabetes, and eventually started losing fingers, toes, and limbs. They cut off the leg above the knee. In the last surgery, they were going to replace her heart valves, so that's how I know about that. They told her she was too weak for the surgery, and they gave her only months to live. Later on, I learned that her cousin faced the same consequences.

Before she died, she came to our house one day and was reading the *Lakota Times* that was on our kitchen table. There was an article that lawyers were helping all of the people who were sexually molested or abused by Catholic priests, nuns, and clergy with a class action lawsuit against the boarding school officials. My relative read the article and said, "**Leksi** (uncle), I have a story I want you to write for me." She said, "Remember that time when I brought you those rolls in the orchard?" Long story short, she and that girl cousin would go to the boarding school, and a Catholic priest would sodomize them before he would give them those rolls. She looked down and cried as she told the story. It made me feel bad. The Spirit, mind, and body can be strong, but when there is trauma, our Spirit gives into disease and sickness. It makes us weaker. It's that kind of negative energy that she took from the experience, the unresolved trauma and grief that she carried. Her mom was a boarding school brat, who beat her with a broomstick until it broke. My relative didn't want to cry from her mom's beating, so her mom got a coffeepot cord and beat her even harder. I begged my relative to cry so her mom would stop, but she wouldn't. Her birthday just passed, so we sat the other night and sang a prayer song for her. She sacrificed a lot for donuts and rolls for us. I hope that wherever she is, she is taking her fill of rolls and donuts without going through the pain she had to endure. I had a lot of anger toward the Catholic priest for a long time.

I cried the whole time, but I wrote up her story in a letter, and it got submitted to those lawyers. In South Dakota these Catholic boarding schools get a lot of money from donors. South Dakota Legislators have created laws to protect the priests and the church. South Dakota doesn't want the church officials to be taken to court for what they did to our youth. What happened to my relative and her cousin was minor compared to what others faced. Another friend of mine had his bones broken, his wrist shredded as a young boy going to boarding school. Later, he hanged himself. He was the basketball coach in his 30s at the local Reservation high school. That's when I started working for the Tribe and began to learn about historical and intergenerational trauma, and all the cases of physical and sexual abuse that occurred, all the things that we went through, and how much it impacted our people. How it continues to control our behavior and contributes to drug and alcohol abuse and early death.

Anyway, I wrote my relative's letter and submitted it. Then we found out we couldn't take the missionaries to court because of South Dakota laws. However, the 1868 Fort Laramie Treaty, which predates South Dakota statehood, has a "No Bad Man" clause, which gives us the right to take them to court, because it happened on Tribal lands. The clause says:

> *If bad men among the whites, or among other people subject to the authority of the United States, shall commit any wrong upon the person or property of the Indians, the United States will, upon proof made to the agent and forwarded to the Commissioner of Indian Affairs at Washington City, proceed at once to cause the offender to be arrested and punished according to the laws of the United States, and also reimburse the injured person for the loss sustained.*

The No Bad Man clause has been successfully used in previous court cases. There was a drunk driver, a non-Indian person, who crashed into a couple on another Reservation and fled the scene. The couple died. The family of the couple took the non-Indian to court and it took a while, but they won. These lawsuits can be an important part of healing to get restorative justice for our peoples.

I heard a story about when Crazy Horse was romancing a lady. Red Cloud told him to go look for buffalos one day with other men, which took him away from the camp for a couple of weeks. During his absence, Red Cloud's nephew No Water approached Crazy Horse's girlfriend's father, requesting marriage. The nephew brought many material things, like ponies, and he was also an accomplished warrior that the father liked. The father accepted this marriage proposal. Before Crazy Horse could return, the pipe ceremony of marriage was completed. When Crazy Horse returned, he went looking for his girlfriend and the father said, "She's married now." Months later, the new husband went on a buffalo hunt. While he was gone, Crazy Horse eloped with this woman who was upset that her father married her to someone else. After two weeks, her husband came back and found that his wife was gone. He went looking for her. Someone told the new husband that his wife left with Crazy Horse. This angered the man because it was his wife by the pipe. When he found them, he shot Crazy Horse in the face. In those days, the guns had a lot of gunpowder and smoke. The bullet entered and exited his jaw and knocked Crazy Horse backward. The man grabbed his wife and left, thinking that Crazy Horse was dead, but he had survived. Because Crazy Horse broke universal law of marriage, Red Cloud and his elite warriors went to Crazy Horse's camp and took his most prized trophy, his war shirt, that shows all the accomplishments he had completed as a warrior. Red Cloud took this away publicly, which shamed Crazy Horse. So Crazy Horse lived in the Bad Nation for a while. From that time until the time he died, he was trying to regain his honor by chasing the goldminers out of the Black Hills and other great deeds. That's how people could earn their way back. To me, the way I understood this scenario, Crazy Horse was the leader of many after having been an outcast to the Bad Nation, because he worked to regain his honor and he demonstrated humility. My grandfather, and many others who didn't want to assimilate, joined Crazy Horse to stand up for our sacred land, the Black Hills.

I think that one of the universal laws that is hardest today for us to digest is humility, but because there has been so much historical trauma it has been difficult for us to let go of anger. Anger is one of the stages of grief that people experience after trauma occurs. When someone is hanging on to anger, it makes it difficult to forgive. We can't be humble if we can't forgive. Forgiveness starts first with self, and then we can forgive others. For many centuries, the Lakota/Dakota/Nakota have lived a life of balance and harmony with Mother Earth. It was the practice of peace and unconditional love for all life-giving energies. The first exposure to Europeans was the introduction of weapons of war and the imbalance of nature through greed. The understanding of being humble remained only with those people who healed by continuing to practice the way of prayer and ceremony.

Birgil Kills Straight led a Big Foot Memorial Ride beginning in 1987 and ending in 1990 to support the Wiping of Tears for the survivors of the Wounded Knee massacres, which had occurred 100 years earlier. I took part because I am a survivor through my grandparents. Many people did not want to wipe their tears, so they were not completed. Those who rode in the ride helped increase the understanding of the healing and mending that needs to take place. Wounded Knee is only one tragedy among thousands that we haven't healed from and let go of yet. I look at the statistics of the abuses of our women and children and it shows me that we have not yet healed. I can also tell that we have not healed because of the nine Sundances in the community I was raised in. Without forgiveness there is no unity.

I still want justice for what was done to our people as many of us do, but I am humbled by Gandhi, who was committed to nonviolent action. Gandhi said, "An eye for an eye leaves the whole world blind." We must stop trying to poke out each other's eyes, be humble and forgive, in order for us to heal Mother Earth for our survival.

One month after my older cousin passed away in 2007, he came to my house, and his Spirit was allowed to pound on the door that shook the whole house and woke me up. I answered the back door and here it was my cousin. He said, "I will come back to help you raise your daughter and son." I said, "If you do, you are going to scare them. You need to go back where you came from." I walked out the back door and said, "I'll go with you so far." We went up a hill and right on top of this hill was a huge valley with a lot of pine trees and a winding river that was at the base. Across that valley was a huge encampment of tipis. I walked with him to the edge of the river. There were men, women, and children in the camp. Beyond the camp were horses grazing and, beyond that, the mountain. I stopped at the edge of the river when I saw the low fog and told him I couldn't go any farther. "You have to go by yourself," I told him. One more time he said, "I want to come and help you." I told him no, that he was needed elsewhere. He gave me a hug. While crossing the river he kept turning to look for me. He did this several times, and I used my hand to motion him to keep going. When he was partway across the river, there were women who came from camp and sat down on buffalo hides on the bank. One of the women who saw my cousin coming said, "***Misun***" (younger brother). All the women turned to see him coming. They were all giving him nurturing energy. When he was still here on earth, he drank. One day when he was drinking, he told his son that he got sodomized when he was very young by one of our relatives when the relative was drinking. When I heard that, it was like a volcano inside of me. I learned that after I had already forgiven the relative for other things. That's when the anger came back to me, again. Now I realize that my relative did everything he could to keep my cousin quiet. I know now my cousin is in a happier place. I turned around and walked back. There was my house. Then I woke up. It was like a dream, only I don't think it was a dream. I think my Spirit that did that. **Mitakuye Oyasin**.

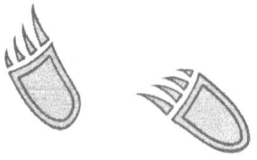

Wokiksuya
(In Memory Of)

Memorial

*I*N MEMORY OF MY RELATIVES and all of our relatives who suffered trauma and abuse at the hands of the missionaries and government boarding school officials. May you be happy, enjoying the *Wo*, with all of those relatives who are on the other side, enjoying good family and love.

Wakanyeja Ota Wokakijapi
(Many Youth Are Suffering and Lost for Not Being Grounded with Proper Protocol)

Teachings about Suicide

*I*N THE LATE 1950s AND EARLY 60s, our youths were attempting suicide at rates higher than non-Tribal communities, just like they are still doing today. Youths were trying to use suicide as the exit to life, entrance into the Spirit World. Some attempted without really wanting to die. In the physical world they felt insecurity or not being loved enough. I think when a youth is pill-popping and cutting, they are looking for attention. They don't cut deep enough, just enough to get your attention. They don't take a lot of pills, just enough to get your attention. Some mess up and end their life by accident. The ones who take lethal methods, they are the ones in whom the Spirit falls out of love. The ones who really mean to kill themselves believe their only answer is in the Spirit World. It might be they are trying to get closer to a grandma who passed on who cared for them. Maybe their parents never picked up caring for them after grandma died. Their Spirit is lonely and sad, looking for that love. In our beliefs, if they shorten their life there is a waiting period in which they could be caught between the worlds. When a person kills themself, their Spirit will go back to the places where they found happiness and love when they were alive. They will go visit those places because the energy of love and memory is still there. The Spirit will hang around that area, crying.

Many believe that if a person dies in a car wreck, the Spirit will stay there and will cry there, too, because there is no love or happiness for them there. People who hitchhike say, "If you walk from this town (where alcohol is sold) to your home, you hear Spirits crying in the ditches." So many died of alcohol-related wrecks on the road from where the alcohol was sold. Today, we have many roads that have a lot of deaths from alcohol or drugs. There used to be a lot of healing and sobriety walks to raise awareness of those relatives who passed on those highways to remind us of the need to return to healthy ways of life.

In our Sundance there is a song about a woman who commits suicide to go to the man she loves. It's hard to explain. When the song is sung, some women hear it and get excited. They say, "There's a woman's song," and they will run to the drum and help sing. The words go, "The man that I love so much is gone, and I care so much that I'm going to be with him." She sings that 4 times, and then on the last time she jumps off a cliff backwards. In one way, it's showing true love. On the other hand, it's foolish. On the foolish side, what if you have kids? Who is going to be hurting more? In a way, that glorifies suicide, and I don't want to glorify suicide because of the current use of alcohol and drugs, and the non-grounding of our people who are lost makes it more likely for them to attempt it.

There was not much education for us about suicide when I was young, except the occasional grandmother's **Wowahokunkiya** (spiritual advice for survival). We did get messages from some church groups that said, "That's [suicide] bad, you're going to go to hell," but that served to scare more than provide education.

When we have trauma and we don't want to feel, we find ways to numb ourselves by turning to drugs and alcohol. It's also a method of suicide.

Woawanglakapo
(Cherish Your Spirit)

Energy of Greed

*T*HERE IS AN ENERGY that we grew up with that we had to learn. It's called greed. It came across the ocean. This energy says, "I've got to have more land, more things, in order for me to be happy."

When I was an undergrad student in Mitchell, South Dakota, I wanted to take a course that would help our Native people. At the time, they didn't have Native studies, so I studied American History. The more courses I took, the sicker and sadder I got. Especially when I got to the Federalist Era that uncovered all that was done to our people. After learning these things, a person might feel like ending their life by suicide or simply getting super angry and engaging in a lot of criminal behavior toward the oppressor. No wonder so many of our people are in prison or six feet under. Where else are they going to exit from this anger?

I quit my American History to live a healthier life. I had to! Soon, American Indian Studies started popping up in college curriculums, and eventually it became a major area of study for me. The people that helped us develop American Indian Studies programs at Dakota Wesleyan University were Jewish. They were doctors at the university who were well educated and could help us, because they could relate to what we had gone through, because of what they'd experienced with the Holocaust in Germany. I'm glad I took those courses in American Indian Studies, even though in the early days (and even still sometimes today), they were taught by White people. White people teaching us about who and how we are. I always wanted to create a course called White Studies so we could tell White people about who and how they are, tell them our stories about what they created. The anger and the sickness that was made.

In Lakota teaching, you can give away material things because they always come back. This comes from the belief in Spirit teachings, **Woawanglaka** (to nurture and love your Spirit), your connection to that invisible world. How you walk in this world is very vital and precious. With that comes honor and respect. The opposite of that is the greed of being selfish and hoarding material wealth, which does not make you a human (living) being.

From a Lakota belief, those who accumulate wealth would share their wealth. One of the three given names of my mother's father was, *Let Them Have Enough.* He was also **Minneconju**, which means Those Who Plant By The Water. He was given this name, Let Them Have Enough, because of his generosity. He was acknowledged by the people with that name because he gave what he had to the people. It makes me proud that I have a grandfather who has that name.

The normal acceptance of a person with wealth among the Lakota was a person who had many more material things than they needed. When someone accumulates more wealth than they need, they lose their humanness. Where are they going with all those things? They are not taking them to the Spirit World. What happens to their Spirit under all those material things they collect?

Lakota families would say humorously, "We are going to dig a hole big enough," when referring to burying a relative who is selfish, so there is room enough for all of their material things to go with them. Those material things really don't matter so much from a Lakota perspective because they are not living. The relatives helped each other live, so life was the most valued energy and was respected over all material things. We never had poor people and rich people in our community because everyone was equal, and everyone shared what they had.

When a person puts material things over human life, it creates a shell of a person. They are not human anymore. The superior spiritual way of thinking is the understanding and relationship we have with all living energy as our family. With that frame of mind, how we respect life and how we take life is sacred. Nothing should be wasted when an animal is killed for us to live. A prayer, an offering of tobacco should be made in thanksgiving for that animal who sacrificed their life for us to live.

How can you live in peace when you are greedy? Along with greed came war, domination, sadness, and despair, even for the greedy ones.

Lakota believe that working with the Spirit is the way to healing. To heal from the anger and the greed, we have to heal the Spirit. We have to go to the ceremony and let go (releasing).

Alcohol and drug treatments are just a Band-Aid because you are not dealing with the problem of the trauma to the Spirit. Today there are more Sweat Lodges and cultural teachings included in some of our treatment centers. This is good. We need more of this!

Woawanglakapo (masculine) **Woawanglakape** (feminine) means to take care of your Spirit or honor your Spirit.

Wicokuja Na Woakipa
(THE SICKNESS OF THE PEOPLE)

Historical Trauma Creates
Our Current State

*I*N 2003, WHEN I STARTED WORKING for the Children's Court, the communities were being very affected by the rising number of youth suicides, which is related to substance abuse because youth under the influence are more likely to attempt to end their life, as compared to when they are sober. Suicide and substance-related deaths are not just an epidemic but a pandemic, as suicide disparities exist for Indigenous communities around the globe. Many people might like to think we have a substance abuse problem, but what we have is a mental and spiritual health problem. The alcohol and drugs numb the mental, emotional, and spiritual pain our people are in. There were three substance-related deaths of youth last week in one of our Lakota communities—two were suicides and one burned in a house fire. It's really bad in some communities now. They are using used plastic water bottles to fill with bootleg alcohol to sell to anyone that wants it, no matter the age. Some Tribes have been declaring a State of Emergency because of how bad the situation is with the drugs, alcohol, and suicide.

Multiple federal policies were enacted to further the mission to *Kill the Indian and Save the Man* (motto of the Carlisle Indian Boarding School, the first). The first boarding school was administered by a military general called Pratt. The military was teaching our youth, beating the Lakota out of us. These policies created more division within the Lakota, and as I meet people from other Tribes they know it was the same result for them, too. As one example, there is an ongoing division of blood quantum **Iyeska** (breed or mixed blood) that resulted from the various Indian Rolls. These rolls, in which Tribal people were required to sign up, represent a termination policy designed to document that there are no more Indians left over time. The intent behind this policy was to eventually remove the obligation of the federal government's trust responsibility to Indians under the rationale that there are no more Indians left as the blood quantum continues to reduce (change) over time. The rolls also diluted the spiritual energy of our people. Now, instead of the Spirit guiding us, the body (blood) has become more important. Today, we carry Tribal cards that list our blood quantum. There are only three sacred beings in the Animal Nation that must document their blood with pedigree papers: dogs, horses, and us. It's like these cards say we don't have a Spirit. We are only a body and can be measured by a quantum of blood. This opens the door for Indigenous people to be treated like animals, to have dominion over. Animals are also a sacred part of the Animal Nation and we should treat them better. As the two-legged species of the Animal Nation, Certificate Degree of Indian Blood (CDIB) also further divides us as humans. The full bloods from the mixed bloods, the dark skins from the light skins, the urbans from the rez dwellers. Dividing us all is the aftermath of the negative energy that has been ruling our lives. Even if we want to be rid of it, even if we want positive energy in our life, we have been unable to free ourselves from the grasp of the negative energy hanging on to us.

A watchdog group from the federal government that was originally housed under the Department of War, and is now under the Department of the Interior, is called the BIA (Bureau of Indian Affairs). It was created to manage the "Indian Problem," and agents of the BIA were directly involved in attempts to suppress the uprising of Native Americans who were banding together to fight for treaty rights. This resulted in massacres, such as Wounded Knee in 1890. We also know that in the 1960s, supporters of the American Indian Movement (AIM) were targeted and taken out (murdered), and in the 1970s, the government turned our own people against us by providing guns to Oglala Lakota people, called the GOONs (Guardians of the Oglala Nation), which became known as the Goon Squad.

At every turn, the federal government was attempting genocide, even turning us against ourselves as one of the most effective strategies. Boarding school, missionary, and government policies created a cumulative anger and fire within many Indigenous people that is difficult to put out. People wonder why there is the "angry Indian." Well this is why. Our people are still traumatized by historical and present day policies and practices meant to destroy us.

If you look at the inappropriate behavior being modeled, it goes way back, and that historical trauma has really done a number on our people. Today, many of our parents don't know how to raise kids. Many people get an attitude when you are trying to change a negative behavior that they have accepted. That's very sad. Some won't look to healing because they have become so accustomed to that lifestyle. I call it survival. That's the only way to survive today. Some sell drugs, some get commodities, some get food stamps, and they all live in the same house to make it work. That's survival. If you try to upset that norm, you become the enemy. But the Healing of our people must take place for the world to survive in the future.

When families are stuck in this "survival for today only" mode, sometimes the only thing that works is the court. Court-ordered parent education. Isn't that something? That is what is happening now among our Tribal courts. This is the era of hollering at your family members just like you (or your grandparent or your great-grandparent) learned in boarding school. That was the trauma that was done to our people and our people are used to that now. Few can settle a family dispute without hollering and using violent physical behavior on one other. A lot of families do this, which traumatizes the kids and creates more disunity among us. Once we got the judge to start court-ordering parents to attend the parent-teacher conference, it worked. Before that, we provided a meal and only 5–6 parents would show up, mostly grandmas and grandpas raising these kids. I look for a word that is really gentle. How do you tell a group of people what is wrong with them in a good way? There are many negative stories of abuse in our family histories, but few teachings of positive parenting skills, such as love, nurturing, bonding, and other qualities that it takes to have a balanced Nation. But even if we don't hear those good teachings, we have those good teachings within us, and it's time to bring them back, to return to our Blueprints.

I pray, pray in sweats, in a good way. The point I'm trying to get across here is prayer. We can start to open up the **Hocoka** and begin to heal through prayer.

The forced indoctrination of Christianity has resulted in varying families or individuals who believe in one of the many Christian missionaries that are on our Reservations. With the increase in Lakota spiritual **Hocokas** that have suddenly risen in our communities, the disunity is still there. In my experience working with our communities, no matter how much we may try with positive energy, the negative always tries to match it. So, we still have the same problems. It's still here.

Today, youth carry real fear of being bullied by gangs, so that negative energy is out there even if a youth wants to avoid it and you are trying to protect them. But it's out there in our communities. One student said they can buy any kind of drug they want at one of our missionary schools, and there are many more like that. The unhealthy lifestyle is taking control of our culture and our spirituality, so much so that now spiritual leaders are using drugs and alcohol. I don't feel good about spiritual people who are using alcohol or drugs being on that hill (Bear Butte) or taking part in any ceremony there.

There is a spiritual leader in our community saying he is sacred. He's been an alcoholic all his life, and he has not stopped. I have heard a lot of bad things about him raping young girls. On a Reservation in Montana, the police escorted him and his father to the border and told them not to return. Victims came forward about him, and they put us on the spot at an elder meeting. We sat through that and listened to that trauma in detail, which was described by his accusers. We advised them to go to the federal authorities, which they did. They said that this individual and his father were trying to start a Sundance on Rosebud. We sent a letter asking this man to come and address what was being said against him. He never showed. We don't support his endeavors on Rosebud anymore. So that's the end of that one for us, but he's now moved on to another community. There are a lot more like him.

I was invited by the Tribe to be a keynote speaker at a day for honoring elders. The majority in the audience were not elders. I made reference that I did not come to speak as a Medicine Man or someone who has power but as a humble common man. During my early years of teaching, both sides of my family were Medicine Men. I was exposed to the ceremony, and I grew up with it. After my father died, and six years in a church school, I never lost my connection to who I am, but I never lived it until I woke up again in 1985. **Kikita** (Awakening). I woke up. I used the term **Lecala Kikita**, which means that I recently woke up. There are a lot of us that go through that. A lot of us just recently woke up. You must respect that awakening and be humble to what you know and what you don't know. The most important thing during this time is to listen and not criticize others.

At the Cannonball (Standing Rock) protest (April 2016–Feb. 2017) of Dakota Access Pipeline (DAPL), there was a young man who came in from Texas claiming to be a Tribal member of Rosebud. He wanted to take over the Sweat Lodge and run the sweat the way he wanted to run it. He tried to get a Sundance started at Cannonball, in the wintertime! Wow! It shows an example of people creating chaos who are not listening and learning proper protocol. There are many types that include Tribal members on Tribal lands who have not been raised with proper teachers or protocols; Tribal members in urban areas who have no teachers and call themselves spiritual leaders; and non-Tribal people who claim to be spiritual leaders who are in our urban cities and rural America. Without these proper teachings and protocols, they are affecting unhealthy behavior that furthers the sickness.

Under the relocation program in the 1960s, a lot of our relatives went off to the cities. Many of the children of these people also just woke up and realized they are Lakota/Dakota/Nakota, so they started reading books and learning more about who they are, which is a good thing. We should encourage them to learn and return to their ways. They may want to be **Wakan** spiritual leaders, but we have to follow teachings and protocol for that to happen. If we do it in a good way, it is not suffering. There are also some things, some protocols, that we will never learn in a city or from a book. We must learn them from a good teacher in the environment (Mother Earth) that we come from. Sacred sites and sacred places.

Somewhere in the Southwest, one or more White men were involved in a money scam. They were charging people enormous prices to attend their sweats, up to $20,000, and calling it a "warrior sweat." They most likely learned about sweat from a book, and then bragged about who taught them or whom they know. At the core, it was a money scam because true and authentic sweats occur at no charge to people who need them, with the underlying norm that those who attend the sweat will give what they can to the Sweat Leader and his helpers, as a part of their **Wopila** (Thanksgiving). There are costs for running a sweat, of course, but they are never charged to the people. A healthy donation, however, is always accepted as a way to support the healing of the people.

The fatal consequences of this money scam were not to the pocketbook, but to the 3 people who died and the 19 who were seriously injured (physically, mentally, and spiritually). Many people participating in these warrior sweats wanted to get out, but the White leaders shunned them and put them down. They looked at a Sweat Lodge as a torture chamber instead of a healing place. That is not our way!

On a humorous note, one of my relatives told me a story about another sweat. The water pourer heard someone fart really loud in sweat, and he yelled, "20 dippers," and didn't allow the door to open. [Laughter] Then at the end of 20 dippers, the person purposely farted again, and the water pourer said, "20 more dippers." [More laughter]. I think the water pourer was trying to get respect from the participants by telling them not to fart, but the participants did not respect him because he wasn't being an authentic spiritual leader. The spiritual leader pouring water was trying to punish this individual but, in doing so, he also impacted the other people who had to endure the heat while these two continued to battle out their respect and disrespect of one another. I think if the water pourer was trying to make a lesson, then he should have let everyone out of the sweat and had a one-on-one with this serial farter. Because he was not an authentic spiritual person, he made everyone suffer. That's not healthy.

In one Tribe I worked with, two Council members would not support the word "spiritual" when referring to traditional people. Our traditional people have always been spiritual. What happened? Fake medicine people are what happened!

My family's spiritual teachers taught me that I had to have nine years of praying and Sundancing before I could pour water in the sweat. There are no hard and fast rules, but this is what I was taught. In other families, people may be allowed to pour water after only a few years.

With proper teachings there is proper protocol. When a Sweat Lodge is built for the people to use, the ***Tiopa*** (door) is wide open. However, it is good to ask permission first before you use someone's place of prayer. It is important that there not be any negativity around a Sweat Lodge for those participating and for those helpers around, as it changes the energy.

If I am being strict about it, and I am these days, it's because I was taught that the Sweat Lodge was made for men, not for women. Before the Europeans arrived, there were no mixed-gender Sweat Lodge ceremonies. The Sweat Lodge is for purification. Originally, women purified through the monthly ceremony, and they did not attend the Sweat Lodge during their menstrual cycle, so they did not hurt themselves or other people. After the second rite of passage when a woman no longer has a monthly cycle, ***Apo*** was used. Apo is a one-door steam where women only use 7 rocks. In the past, the men's sweats used only 7 rocks because the Sweat Lodge was built only for maybe three or fewer people, and the lodges were covered with one buffalo hide. Only 7 rocks were needed because people were practically sitting over those rocks in these old-time sweats.

While it is difficult to know what happened before and after Europeans arrived, I believe that the 4-door sweat is a result of the historical trauma and the need to heal the blood from post-traumatic stress. As the Lakota men got blood on their hands, they needed (4) doors to heal themselves. Today, because the Sweat Lodges are covered with canvas and can be larger, more rocks are needed, and these 4-door sweats have remained. Women are also using these same methods, and today there are also some who practice coed sweats. Sometimes this is a reality of the lack of available spiritual leaders (male/female) who can run separate sweats, and sometimes it is the result of the isolation that occurred when we were placed in remote Reservation Prisoner of War camps. While many may not know this, Reservations were first called Prisoner of War Camps, and we had a number assigned to us.

It's also important to know that it is not the heat that is healing but the prayers within.

Women Sundance today, too. I was taught that Sundance is a men's ceremony. The only woman involved in the Sundance is a virgin child, symbolizing the **Pte San Win** (White Buffalo Calf Woman). This virgin girl helped cut the tree down and is the only one inside the Sundance circle for the first entrance. Then she leaves. In the evening she comes back in the circle again and exits with the men. She didn't dance all day long.

People say, "I'm a Sundancer."

The question is, "How long have you been Sundancing?"

Those are some of the anxieties I deal with daily. My anxiety is that young people pick up things quickly. When they pick up things quickly, they can cause more problems because they didn't learn enough. Some want shortcuts and instant gratification, which do not exist on the Red Road. They don't know the **Wo** that we are talking about. They don't know about that spirituality. They really think they know it all in 4 years, which is the length of a Sundance commitment.

One year, a confrontation happened with a young person, who was doing his own thing and being very negative when the local leaders asked him to follow the local protocol. Later we learned that this Lone Ranger was also asked to leave another Sundance. Negativity divides people. I could see it coming. I got to a point where I saw that it was a losing battle. Either participants would follow this man and leave, or they would stay. Many chose to stay but some of his relatives left the camp with him. When they left, a mist rolled uphill from the valley. Even though our Sundance was at a higher elevation, you could just see it clearly coming up the road, slow moving. It was a sacred moment. It came up the road and through the campgrounds. It was a thick fog like a cloud. It came to the Sundance circle and made a circular motion like it was smudging or cleansing the whole campground. The whole Sundance was traumatized by what had happened. Everyone was still standing there, the singers and the women with their skirts on. Just as soon as it came, it left, and the sun came out. Someone said, "Let's pray." So, we all went back out to the Sundance tree and prayed. While we were doing that the singers sang a really nice prayer song. It was a sacred moment that brought tears to everyone's eyes. The Sundance still continued that day. We persisted through this negativity.

This disruption from unhealthy behavior seeps into our families and becomes a threat and intimidation of one another, affecting our spiritual ways. It's even hard for many of our families to honor one another and pray together sometimes.

In 1987, I was told to return to the community I grew up in because there was a movement to go back to the old form of government, before the Indian Reorganization Act (IRA, 1934) had taken place, when headmen, called **Naca**, were leaders of the communities. After the IRA, headmen were moved into Council representative positions in the new form of government. At that time, my grandfather Robert Two Elk was a selected **Naca** and transitioned to be a Council representative. He took that position and served for thirty-six years because he continually got re-elected. The movement to go back to the old way of government was supported by a grant, coordinated by Dr. Elgin Bad Wound. He spoke to our elders, and they found out that the last headman there was my grandfather Robert Two Elk. My oldest sister was consulted because she still lived in the community, and she selected me to be the next lineal descendant for that position of **Naca**, or headman. I received a letter to come home on a certain date to have my grandfather's bonnet placed on my head. I was supposed to go back to complete the ceremony and receive that bonnet.

I went a few days ahead of time and the community, being in a very negative way of life, was not unified. I observed a lot of negative energy: fathers against sons, mothers against daughters, brother against brother, sister against sister. A lot of unhealthy behavior. Word got out that I was to receive this bonnet, and I began receiving threats. They even threatened me with death.

As the ceremony started, the elders who were there all took turns speaking. When it came to be my turn, I was unhappy with the way the community was behaving. So, I told them, "I am accepting this honor, but at this time, I am not going to put this bonnet on my head for fear of retribution and harm to me or my family." I took the bonnet and told the community members present that I will return and be their leader when they are ready to heal. Following traditional protocol, as the rightful next heir, I am protecting the bonnet. I hope for the day that I may wear it for the people.

I was working for the government at that time living off my Reservation. What I learned about living in a housing unit was that there was no rest. People were knocking on the door all the time because we had the only phone available to call the ambulance or the police. One day, we went to the store and came back and all of our clothes were stolen from the clothesline. When you are raised traditionally you say, "Well we hope they will be warm with our clothes," and let it go. But the system thrives on us getting mad and reacting, because it makes the colonizer's work easier. The last stage of colonization is when we turn on each other; then the colonizer's job is over because we are doing it for him. Dog-eat-dog world. When alcohol was introduced to our people the sentiment was, "We don't have to kill these Native peoples, we can give them alcohol and let them kill themselves." When the colonizers reach that point of using other forms of genocide, they don't have to feel guilty about killing our people anymore. They introduced alcohol so that we could kill ourselves. Now it's drugs, too. Lawmakers being slow in helping our Indigenous peoples is another form of genocide that often goes unrecognized.

Ten years after the **Naca** ceremony, my house was broken into and my own relatives took the 36 golden eagle tail feather bonnet.

I'm glad I practice our way of prayer. It gives us a gentle way of dealing with those types of people and, in that way, through prayer, things can get better. People reach a time of maturation where they think nothing can be done about it anyway, and that's how people look at things. That is part of the negativity, in believing that nothing can be done about it. Some people accept that "no one is going to do anything about it, so why try." Many have developed a sense of helplessness. This is a big part of the negativity and keeps us from healing in our communities.

If the police are the relatives of someone committing a crime, nothing will happen to them; it is the same with many other professional positions, even the judges. In these cases, when a person is related to someone in power, no justice is served, even when it is rightfully deserved. In other cases, if you are not related to anyone in power, your case may not get any time or attention and, thus, no justice.

Getting justice also requires Tribal laws that will support that justice. Within one of the Tribes I work with, the Juvenile Code hasn't been changed since 1968. Wow! How do children receive justice in today's world with laws that are 50 years old?

We started to create a group of people to amend the juvenile code to fit the behavior of our people today by addressing all of these unhealthy behaviors. One thing that I saw was abandonment, neglect, and abuse. All kinds of abuse! Spiritual, mental, emotional, and physical abuse. I'm glad they have an elder abuse law now, but I'm not sure who is enforcing it. Elder abuse law is there, but elders are still being abused. Just like children.

I'm glad that many Tribes are looking at constitutional reform to get away from the Indian Reorganization Act (IRA) form of government, under which the old practice of having spiritual leaders who care about the people went away. The IRA took the prayer out of leadership. Under our traditional form of government, leaders were selected by the spiritual leaders with approval of the camp because of their capacity and honor in following Lakota values (**Naca**). Leaders were not paid a salary to help the people; the people just took care of them because everyone was cared for. Everyone had food, and everyone was treated equally. There was no child abuse and neglect; abusers were sent to the Bad Nation/ **Oyate Sica**. There were rarely divorces and spousal abuse, also due to the penalty of being sent to the Bad Nation. Violent behavior was not tolerated as it broke universal law. If there was concern among the camp about a person's ability, there was a set protocol that included discussion and examining evidence of the ability. In the case where those concerns were valid, they looked for another leader.

Under the IRA form of government that was forced on us, people started getting paid to do services for the people. Spiritual leaders were no longer included as there was a declaration of the separation of church and state, and everything became individualized instead of collective. Under the IRA form of government, we became a capitalist society, and this teaching was brought to us by the Christians.

In the New International version of the Bible, it says in Genesis 1:28:

> *God blessed them and said to them, 'Be fruitful and increase in number; fill the earth and subdue it. Rule over the fish of the sea and the birds of the air and over every living creature that moves on the ground.'*

This set the stage for domination over other living things, including people of color, and in the Papal Bulls, the Pope wrote the word "domination" as the directive that guided the early explorers. Today, through this IRA form of government, we are living as capitalists, as dominators. There are the haves and the have-nots.

In our traditional way of government, everyone got fed, everyone got housing, everyone got doctoring. In this way, we were the original Socialists or original Communists, but I don't even like to use those English terms because, as soon as we say the word Communist or Socialist, that gives Christians more approval for trying to get rid of us by their self-proclaimed doctrine of discovery and religious beliefs of domination over others under the rule of capitalism, stepping over others for individual gain.

Some say, "That Two Elk . . . he's a troublemaker" because I am challenging their learned behavior that is not healthy.

I have to pray a lot for protection because I'm trying to get our people to change their way of life. Not only our Lakota people need to heal, but there needs to be a global healing of all living energy, including Mother Earth, to turn from domination into the light of God, which is love. Love for ourselves and love for each other, as unique as we all are.

We (Weh) Wojapi
(Mixing of Blood)

Mixed Bloods

WHEN I FIRST STARTED SUNDANCING at Grandpa Fools Crow's, he allowed a little boy and a little girl to lead the morning dance. At the beginning of each morning, we made an entrance, like a grand entry before the sun came up. (The entry represents the ages and stages of life, with the younger people leading and the grandma and grandpa walking behind them.) One Sundance morning, Grandpa Fools Crow selected a mixed blood, a visibly black boy—whose mother was Oglala—as the boy to lead the dance. Some relatives looked shocked and covered their mouths. When the break occurred, Grandpa Fools Crow got on the PA system and spoke Lakota. He advised the people by saying, "I chose this little grandson to come out here because I want to educate you where our people are going and where we are today." We can't deny what we have in our blood, ***Wojapi***. When I say ***Wojapi*** some people think of the pudding, but I'm talking about the mixing of the blood. You cannot deny that because your children's, children's, children are going to be mixed. You will be long in the ground in the spiritual realm somewhere, and you can't do anything about your mixed descendants. In 7 generations your family may be all White or all Black. He spoke about the 4 colors in our Circle: Red, Yellow, Black, and White.

I went to the Foxwoods Resort Casino, owned by the Mashantucket Pequot. I never saw any visible Indians there because they are all mixed. They look Black or White, but they still have their Tribal government and cultural ways. The prophecy says we will all become one race, as our bloods mix, we will all become one and the same.

We ki Wakan
(The Blood is Sacred)

Wakanyeja (Sacred Children)

After trauma, grief, or loss, the Calling the Spirit Back ceremony happened immediately through the *Inipi* (Sweat Lodge), but the Wiping of the Tears was to be completed after 13 moons of grieving. A grieving person needs one year to heal. One year is the respected time for healing, but it may take longer for some who want to continue to grieve. After one year, the community performed a "Wiping of the Tears" ceremony to welcome the healed person back into the Circle of Life.

In our *Wolakota*, we are taking shortcuts. For example, today, grieving and mourning for a loved one who has passed on lasts 4 days after the funeral, when we go through a Wiping of the Tears. Only 4 days after the body is in the ground. So a lot of families still carry unresolved grief issues. And when they are not grieving, the grief is multiplied when there are multiple loses within their community and extended family. We are burying people on a weekly basis. Because they are not grieving, the grief comes out in destructive ways, like alcohol and drug abuse. When people go through the Wiping of the Tears before they've had time to grieve, the ceremony is less effective. You are still in shock 4 days after a loss. One year after a traumatic loss or event, you have a very different perspective and are more ready to Wipe the Tears and fully come back to the community.

One of the contemporary challenges is that those of us who are grieving often must go back to work soon after a loss or traumatic event. If we don't pay bills, we lose things and have consequences, so, many times we must go back to work. The need is there for healing, but the need for the dollar drives us to return to work. But as Lakota we understand that healing process is even more important than the dollar. We must take time to heal. When, as grievers, we don't have time to heal, we come back into the workforce wounded and are likely to have breakdowns, even anxiety attacks, and have accidents or injuries as our Spirit is not there. Post-traumatic stress disorder is also something that occurs under heavy trauma or stress. I found what really helps during this time is the power of prayer and the power of ceremony.

There are many more people these days who don't go through the Wiping of the Tears. Especially in the case where a person passes on. Some individuals or families don't know how to let go of the Spirit or the memory of the person. They may be having memorial dinners or activities thirty years after the person dies. In some ways, this is good to help the living stay motivated to keep helping the people, but there is a time they have to let go because it can be harmful.

There was a family I worked with who had two sons. One of the sons killed himself. He was a ballplayer. After he died, the whole family would raise money all year round to put on a memorial ball game, so much so that all the effort was focused on the memorial, and they didn't focus on the younger living children. The one who committed suicide had more attention from Mom or Dad than those who were living did. Then the living child also considered suicide, and the parents were oblivious. It's almost like the parents were trying to make up for the love they didn't give while their child was alive. The living son told me, "I should kill myself so that

Dad would pay attention to me." This is a good example of how not letting go can become unhealthy.

One day while I was washing dishes, a song came on the radio and I started bawling. Really crying hard. It was the "Ballad of the Green Berets." A good buddy of mine I met at Bear Butte was an Oneida warrior, a decorated veteran with six or seven tours in Vietnam, and he was going through PTSD. So I helped him, but he just couldn't let go of the cocaine. (It eventually took his life.) The song triggered me to remember him, and I shed tears. After socializing with him, he would crank up that song and yell, "There's my song!" This is another example of how unresolved grief will come up when you least expect it. Unresolved trauma, grief, and loss can be triggered by an infinite number of things.

I have seen the non-Indian way of dealing with trauma, grief, and loss. It's not as in-depth. It's not as powerful. The non-Indian way is like a Band-Aid. I don't like that psychotropic drugs are being prescribed so quickly, instead of giving more long-term therapy. We are trying to quick-fix them and put them back into society, as if they don't have a problem. That's why we have so many shooters who turn on innocent people. It's so sad because they never heal. So many people have been traumatized, and all they need is long-term love, healthy love, and they will come out of it to get re-grounded. They don't need psychotropic drugs, but in the immediate, the system will connect them to a psychiatrist and give them drugs to numb their pain. Then they just go on living with it. Like living zombies.

They don't want children to be aggressive at school, so they give them Ritalin, and then the children return to school like zombies. There are many reasons why kids are aggressive or act out behaviorally. We know that this is a sign of a trauma or a grief response in children. Kids don't understand emotions very well yet, so they act out. I bumped heads with superintendents at many schools over this. I've seen these medicated kids coming into the Sweat Lodge where they cry. When you go inside the sweat, you can't run away. That's when you talk to your Spirit. The children cry like little babies because they are little babies. Because of their home environment, they have to create a world to survive. That's where they create that tough side, the aggressive side. By the time the sweat is over, I have them hugging each other. Ceremony breaks down that tough side and allows their ***Tiopa*** (doorway) to open. Every afternoon, the kids would run to my office at the school and ask, "When are we going to have a sweat? When is the next sweat?" For me, it's a good place to help them let go of some of their frustrations, their anger. They are workable. They need long-term therapy, not thirty days or a medication treatment cycle.

Many of our kids are traumatized, which comes off as anger, and that's when they do bad things. Many of them are handicapped with Fetal Alcohol Syndrome/Fetal Alcohol Effects (FAS/FAE) or from developmental delays due to incest. Many of these cases are misdiagnosed as Attention Deficit Hyperactivity Disorder (ADHD) or Conduct Disorder. I call it a double whammy because they are not only traumatized by the alcohol and violence in their family, but also they are living with the fetal alcohol or incest symptoms. Some youth with FAS/FAE are also kids living with the consequences of incest. That's the triple whammy. When one of these children says, "I want to grow up to be a doctor," what do you say to them? You have to prepare the family to help the child, as he or she may be vulnerable to suicide. These are the highly at-risk kids.

"No one around here is related on Friday night" was how the grandma referred to incest and the children being born into this world from incest. I agree with her. That's how it is. There are communities where people drink alcohol and then they lay with each other, and babies are born. In the 1950s, I asked my mom about a pitiful child. She told us to be quiet and put her finger to her lips, "Shhhhh." Afterwards at home, she explained that it was an embarrassment for some families to talk about a child because their father is their uncle. These young people don't know what to do with themselves, and they have limited cognitive ability because of the retardation. So, when the family they love is drinking and commands them to get out of the house, they don't know what to do or where to go. They cry. That family is the only connection they have, and they have love for their family. So, when they are rejected with few skills or resources, they are pitiful. Then later they commit suicide or hurt others out of anger. Those are the ones you find hanging in the trees. Those are the ones who end up in long-term incarceration.

That teaching about the blood was intact in the physical sense before the Christians came. Regarding the blood, our grandmas and grandpas already knew about incest and what happens to the people because of incest, which is why we have included our Northern Cheyenne and the Arapaho as potential mates. We go to them for our spouses to keep the blood without incest. Incest was so frowned on that you couldn't even marry your 13th or 14th cousin. As a young boy growing up, I didn't know that, and I fell in love with a lot of my cousins and shared this with my sisters, who would tell on me. My parents came to me and said, "That's your cousin; you can't do that." So, my heart was broken many times; I had to tear up many love letters, and I had to teach that to my children. My daughter was more upfront with that and would openly tell a boy, "We're related!" When I got older, my mom told me never to marry anyone from the community I grew up in, as I am related to everyone there, in one way or another.

This one young girl, before she committed suicide, she really fixed her face up like she was going to church. She went over the hill and she was gone. The next day someone came looking for her, and she was hanging in the tree. The mother drank, everyone in the home drank. When mom was drunk, the girl was molested and raped. These were the young people I was working with at the Juvenile Detention Center. The police only have the reported cases that are the frosting on the cake, the ones with evidence and willing survivors to report what happened. Most of the abuse is unreported. There are a lot of unhealthy things going on in our homes. I cry for them. I cry for these youths. Parents left them with not only the physical pain but also with the mental and emotional pain of not being loved. I mean not having family love.

There is so much trauma going on. Trauma prevention should be a part of the suicide task force on the Reservation. Our people should be trained to do some type of healing for the mental and emotional side, but the healing of the spiritual side is equally important.

I have seen young parents with no knowledge of raising children try to buy the love of their children through buying expensive gifts that they think will compensate for their absence. Over years, they create a spoiled young adult or adult. When the parent can no longer afford the gifts because the child wants more and more, the child will **Wacinko** (pout). That's when many cases of cutting, overdosing, and accidental suicides occur. They might get drunk and think that someone will cut them down, but no one cuts them down in time and they die. Or they take Tylenol as a pseudo-suicide attempt to get attention of a mother or a boyfriend or girlfriend, thinking it won't hurt them, then their liver fails, and they die.

In one of the cases I worked on, the state took a young girl into custody when it became evident that her grandma was selling the girl's body for sex. Grandma was allowing her granddaughter to be raped so grandma could play bingo and gamble. Oftentimes, the challenges we face are related to unhealthy relatives who are creating this chaos. Sometimes these relatives are on Tribal Council, sometimes they are the local law enforcement officers, and sometimes they are the local Indian Child Welfare Act[5] workers. When sick people are trying to help sick people, the outcome is not good.

Researchers try to study why so many of our youth are killing themselves. I don't have to look far to know why.

---

5   Congress. United States Code: Indian Child Welfare, 25 U.S.C. §§ -1963 1988. 1988. Periodical. Retrieved from the Library of Congress, <www.loc.gov/item/uscode1988-009025021/>.

We brought in the Lakota culture and spirituality, which helped the youth find a safe healthy family while incarcerated at the Juvenile Delinquency Center. No one was fighting in their house at the Juvenile Delinquency Center.

Mitakuye Oyasin
(All My Relatives)

The World's Shortest Prayer

As long as I can remember, *Mitakuye Oyasin* was said after a prayer. It was said out of respect for addressing the people. It was the completion of whatever they were saying. When a person said, "*Mitakuye Oyasin*," it was a sign that they were done. So, then somebody else could talk without disrespecting that person. That concept of being related was my whole understanding. I need to explain that our people were not violent people the way the books have written about us as heathens and savages going around scalping and killing people. We were not like that!

I remember seeing my first black-and-white movie. We saw it at the local school gym on the Reservation. I remember how, when the cavalry came with its horn blowing [horn sound], the whole Lakota community cheered for the cavalry to come to save whomever. So, I remember Vine Deloria Jr. talking about that. That is assimilation: a whole mindset of not really knowing who we are if we cheered for the cavalry in the movie. This is the portrayal of the same cavalry who came to kill our people.

We forgot the original reference to **Mila Hunska** (Long Knives.) **Mila Hunska** caused fear in our people. I made that reference to the Jews regarding the Nazis during the Holocaust. When you say the name *Nazi* it has a profound effect on Jewish people, the same effect that hearing **Mila Hunska** does for our peoples, especially for the ones who actually saw the horror. **Wasin Icu** came later, as White men were observed eating the fat of a pig. **Wasin Icu** means takes (eats) the fat. We Lakota didn't take the fat. We used buffalo fat to waterproof our tipis and other wares, so we wouldn't eat the pig fat. Later on, the philosophy of Takes the Fat was associated with the greed of the white people, and the name stuck with them for Lakota people. The short way to say this is **Wasicu**.

On a side note, the **Kukuse** (pig) had so much fat coming off it that it didn't look healthy like the buffalo fat. It might have had an odor too. Maybe it didn't harmonize with the buffalo hide. I used to think it was a Lakota word, but then I went to the Ojibwa and they were using the same word, **Kukuse**, to refer to pig. I told them I didn't know it was an Ojibwa word and they said it was not Ojibwa, but something they learned from the French. When they were mad at one another they would yell, "**Kukuse**!" across the river. Symbolically, it became a reference to White people because the **Kukuse** eats everything. That's why you feed pigs slop, because they will devour anything, even themselves. No one wanted to be like the **Kukuse**; they thought if you ate the pig you would become like the pig or like the White man. Either way, our people didn't want to eat the fat back then. Today, that has changed cause we learned to love commodity SPAM, for me dipped in mustard [Laughter].

Since I am the youngest of nine children, I feel that my eight sisters and brothers went through a lot more than me. I think my parents learned by raising my siblings. When it came time to raise me, I was treated differently. That's the feeling I get. I think every family is like that. The youngest is exposed to a lot of what the older ones went through. My father tried his hardest to pass to me the oral teachings of my people. So did my mother. Raising me in a way that I can survive. A lot of our stories, like our bedtime stories, have a moral to them. A teaching. I believe that is another way of surviving, so you can understand life and how to survive.

At the same time, you learn to use another medicine for survival. That medicine is laughter. Our humor. Our people were good at humor. We are still good at humor today. It is one form of medicine that has helped us survive, and still helps us! It is always good to hear the aunties, uncles, grandmas, and grandpas laughing. It is good energy in any of our celebrations when we come together. Like the name giving ceremony, honoring, or any time of celebrating achievements when our people gather to feast and honor, there is laughter.

During those times of awareness, a lot of the teasing, joking, and humor occurred; that Lakota medicine (***Pejuta***) of humor or laughter was used to keep that balance. The other ***Pejuta*** is releasing tears through crying. You can get tears from both sadness and happiness. I remember, in my lifetime, I laughed so hard at some humorous things that happened that tears came out. Today, in our spiritual ways, that's also part of our releasing (4th ceremonial part). When you do that releasing there is a feeling of lightness or a lot of weight is taken off your shoulders.

WoInipi
(Through the Mouth You Live Sacred)

Wo
(God's Presence, the Sacred)

I (ee)
(Mouth)

Nipi (neepee)
(To Live)

*I*n 1996, I met a set of twins who experienced FAS. Today they call it FAS/FAE or Fetal Alcohol Syndrome and Fetal Alcohol Effects. I saw this boy who was bringing coffee for the drummer, and he was calling one of the drummers "Grandpa." He was like a little gopher. He would gopher (go for) stuff. He seemed like a little kid, but in reality, he was in his 20s, and his growth was stunted. The grandpa was ordering the young man around very rudely. Everything the grandpa asked of the young man he did, gladly, in a very nurturing way. Then I saw the young man looking toward the bleachers and smiling. That's when I noticed that he had a twin, and that she had the same FAS features that he had, except hers were more severe. I felt bad for the way the grandpa was treating him. I felt bad for these twins. I think about the Spirits in those bodies, and what they must have had to go through.

Yesterday some girls came into the office and asked about plants. I shared with them that the grandmas and grandpas taught us that we used to be able to talk to plants, to animals, to rocks, and to the trees. There was a certain time to plant and a certain time to harvest. When we do things in an appropriate way, at the right time, the food tastes better.

When I was 9 years old we moved to town. As my dad was driving me around town in the pickup truck, he would tell me about homes not to go to because this person had **Wicokuja** (bad, unhealthy, or unnatural energy). He would say, "Don't play with the kids that come from this home." The way my mom raised me, she was kindhearted and had pity for people. She was not as tough as my dad. My dad was very tough in showing me what homes not to go to and explaining to me that these homes had sickness, as a reason why I shouldn't go there. When my dad talked to me about the sickness in the homes it included those with physical, mental, emotional, or spiritual illness.

In the past, parents, grandparents, or guardians did not allow negative energy to be around children. They know that a negative person can create disharmony or overwhelm innocent children to lead them down the dark path, so they become like the negative person. When we had relatives who were known to be negative people, we weren't allowed, as toddlers, to climb all over them. We would be put in a different room. But they would let us play with positive people. In the past, those relatives who could not conform to universal laws, if they were abusive, they were warned. If they did not change, they were taken to the edge of camp and told to leave. These outcasts slowly gathered to create another camp called the Bad Nation. When I was growing up and we moved to town, my mom and dad told me to not go to an uncle who came from prison because he'd killed a man out of anger, not in battle.

There is a difference. Anything he touched, especially food, they said not to take. If you did, you were going to be like him. His energy was going to rub off on you, or **Woayapi**. I never accepted anything my uncle tried to give me to eat or drink. I would give an excuse and run home.

The grandpas and grandmas reminded us that, with good energy, everything we do is good or healthy. In the traditional way, when you visit someone's home, they offered you food or drink. The grandpas and grandmas would eat one another's food when visiting. Through the eating of food in that home, they would observe what kind of energy the home had. They knew right off the bat if it was a happy home or a sad home. If it was a sad or unhealthy home, they made an excuse to leave. They gave some excuse and left right away. They would treat the people like relatives and were hospitable to them, but if they sensed bad energy, they would get out quick. If actions are fake, a wise grandparent can see behind that mask into how you're feeling. They know! The grandmas and grandpas know when someone is happy and when someone is unhappy. They can tell it in the food. If the food doesn't taste good, like if the potatoes are hard or something, they know that person's heart is not in the right place to be cooking. There is a reason that people burn things, scorch things—they know all that. They know that when someone has a happy, stable home, the food tastes good and the energy is good.

The **Inipi** (Sweat Lodge) is a powerful practice for healing the body, mind, and Spirit to cleanse the negative energy. It helps an individual be strong and healthy. Water is the gift of life to all living energy on Mother Earth. The rock is the representation of the energy that created us, **Inyan** (Creator/Grandfather Rock). **Inyan** comes into the **Inipi**, and when water is poured on it creates another energy called **Apo** (steam), that is positive energy to take negative energy out of our body through our sweat glands and help our minds and Spirits through prayer and song. A reasonable amount of steam is healthy and can help you achieve a cleansing (feeling lighter), but too much steam can be harmful.

I have witnessed injury by "plastic" Medicine Men running Sweat Lodges and creating disharmony with our sacred ways, such as women being raped in the lodge. This is not good!

Some who pour water and do not check for first timers, will run it extra hot and chase these people away. They, the young and first timers, leave believing the *Inipi* is a torture chamber and do not return.

Some who pour water may not know that their tolerance level for heat is very high, and they expect everyone to be at their level of tolerance. So, they pour the water on, even dumping the bucket of water on the hot rocks. Where is their *Waunsila* (unconditional love or having pity for one another)? Having pity for those who want to learn how to pray is not to cause fear and have them run away and never return again. Some make it extra hot in the *Inipi*, mistakenly believing that the hotter it is, the closer you are to God. This is not so!

Mitakuyepi (my relatives), if you are going to teach, teach in a good-hearted way. *Cante waste ya waunsila yuha mani po* (With these teachings treat everyone with a good heart). I thought I would never reach the age of giving advice; when I was growing up, I always thought of advice givers as crabby old people. However, here I am, a crabby old person giving advice [Laughter], and I am grateful to be here today giving it.

It is not good for those who have one to four years of walking with the *Canupa Wakan* to give advice, or holler at elders who have more years of experience. We should respect our elders.

My elders told me that the *Inipi* was made for men. Women only *Apo* (steam) themselves a little because of their sacredness. *Wakanyeja* (sacred children) are *Wakan* (holy/sacred) and do not need the full *Inipi* ceremony, unless they are being doctored by a proven Medicine Man. *Wakanyeja* do not need purification, they are already pure, innocent.

In my learning about the *Inipi,* I was burned out of one, and when I was leaving the person running the lodge called me a wimp, a chicken, and other words that I won't say in this book. If

I did not love my **WoLakota** ways, I would have not ever tried the ***Inipi*** again. I found out later that the person who burned me out, learned how to run a Sweat Lodge in prison. He had killed a man and was serving time when he learned this way.

I look at it like a terrorist approach. The ones who really practice some of our ways, learn it from being in prison. There are no drugs or alcohol in prison so you go deeper inside yourself, being isolated from the chaotic world outside. You may gain a better understanding while you're in prison, but when you get out, there may not be anyone out there who is practicing the proper protocols to allow you to continue these ways while you rehabilitate. One must be respectful of why they were placed in prison because the outside world, those who they hurt, still have a negative label for them when they get out.

I shared about the Bad Nation and that one of the ways to get back into the circle is to regain your honor by completing positive acts for the camp. Depending upon the severity of why a person was asked to leave, they may be allowed to do the dragging of the skull outside the Sundance circle to be welcomed into the circle of the camp again. Children may throw rocks at them during this time to see if they will get angry. In this way the person is tested to see if they have enough humility to return. You are not allowed to come back in the circle if you continue your improper behavior.

Those customs are still observed, but it's hard to go back to the old ways because the old ways have stronger discipline in how you approach spirituality. We have so many things going on today for people to find the proper person that they want to pray with. That is why we have so many mixed Sundances. There are mixed ceremonies going on now that some people are happy with, and some are not. I try to teach my family some of the things that we need to hang on to maintain our way of life, our spiritual belief, and to attract and bond with other people with similar feelings in prayer. It is hard to advise others on the old teachings without retribution or negative consequences. Because people were not exposed to the old teachings, they don't see or understand them.

I serve as an elder in many roles, and serious situations and problems are brought to us often. As one example, there are certain individuals who are not following proper protocols—false medicine people, false Christians—and doing harmful things. I guess it's been going on for so long now it's hard to have our people, as a whole, go back to the old ways, the old teachings, because everyone has their own value system, their own belief system now. Our energies have become fractionated because of all of the different belief systems that are making an individual say, "No, this is the right way, follow me, follow me." That has carried over to the Sundance circles and it's why we have so many Sundances; the same goes with Sweat Lodge, and I have told you about all of the churches and missionaries on the Reservations.

There are so many transitions (fractions) going on in our spiritual communities that you can lose your connection to **Tunkasila**. Every time there is a gathering, you know what the people ask today: "Do they feed?" The desire to eat had become more important than the prayers and gathering with the people. When the people come, how many are truly listening to resolve the reality we face? Are they there in their mind and in their Spirit or are they just eating? Before you are even done with your speech, they are gone. We are like mosquitos now, we eat to get our fill, and we fly off.

I shared with you that the **Inipi** (Sweat Lodge) symbolizes the mother's womb where you communicated as a Spirit to the Grandfathers. When you are in the **Inipi**, you are a Spirit in the womb, just like you were as an unborn fetus. That Spirit (7th direction) has the option to stay or leave. While you are in the womb, your Spirit is coming and going for the 9 months your mother is carrying you. Your Spirit knows and hears the mom and dad's thoughts. If the Spirit is not being loved, the Spirit will not stay. That baby's Spirit, your Spirit, is the 7th direction, so that direction is where that Spirit is, wherever that might be, in the womb, in the earth world, or in the Spirit World.

In the ***Inipi*** everyone must practice the universal laws of unconditional love or ***Waunsila*** (having pity for one another), ***Wacante Ognake*** (generosity from the heart), and ***Wowacintanka*** (fortitude).

I was told to observe those who pour water for ***Inipi*** and see what kind of energy they possess. Some people should not pour water because they do not have the right energy for it.

If the balance of one who is pouring water is negative, they will cause more damage than good in the ***Inipi***. Every negative thought, word, or deed can spoil an ***Inipi***.

Do not take negative energy into the ***Inipi***, not even a single thought. Whatever your heart wishes, it will happen. If you do not believe, then nothing will happen, because you doubt yourself. If you produce negativity, you will make it happen, and it will also come back on you. What goes around, comes around. You must be careful what you think, what you say, and what you do. This is similar to the Eastern idea of Karma.

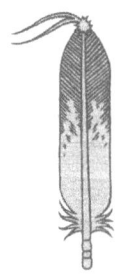

Hunka
(Making Relatives)

[This topic of Hunka, Making Relatives, was presented across various sacred sites in Guatemala as Tokala, others, and I supported an international exchange for healing that included Indigenous leaders from North, Central, and South America. One morning during this visit in Chimaltenango, Guatemala, we had some free time, and we asked two young men if we could accompany them to the market. After a strange glance between them, they agreed. When it was time to leave, they gave us each a coin in Quetzales (local currency). We assumed they were going to drive, so we didn't understand why they were giving us money. But we went along anyway, as we do when we can't speak the same language, and soon realized that the money was for a bus fare. It was 8:00 a.m. on a Monday when we boarded an incredibly colorful LED-lit Guatemalan bus that was so packed a Maya woman felt the need—and the right—to sit on Tokala's lap. We could not help but laugh as we were crammed on the bus like sardines in a can. There were literally men and women standing on the ledge outside of the bus holding on like pirates to the mast of a schooner on a raging sea as the bus driver attempted to dodge the ever-common potholes on the streets used by the common people. When it was our stop we squeezed

by other passengers while I pleaded, "por favor, discúlpame" (please excuse me in Spanish); we were swimming through the bodies like we were fish. Freedom at last! We laughed and tried to walk together as quickly as a group of foreigners and locals could, to arrive at the people's market. However, Tokala looked funny, how he was walking, and he was having a very difficult time keeping up. In these days of 2018, he did not use a cane and walked mostly by himself. One of the Maya relatives, trying to figure out what problem Tokala was having with walking, yelled, "Tokala's zapata's zapata's!" (which means shoes in Spanish). As he summoned our attention to Tokala's feet, we all noticed his shoes were on backwards. We laughed so hard that tears fell from many eyes that day. We stopped for a seat under an overpass so Tokala could switch his shoes. This was a funny moment of bonding laughter for all of us, including Tokala, who finally figured out, also, why he was having such a difficult time walking. It was also the moment we realized Tokala needed a little more support with his vision, so we all began to cross the physical boundaries that are customary in our communities to help him a little more. What a wild visit to the people's market we had that day! Rows and rows of fresh produce, barrels full of shrimp, fresh cheese wrapped in banana leaves, buying, selling, and trading for ceremonial supplies of fragrant herbs and flowers, beeswax candles, sticks from pine, papaya, cocoa, and baby fruits. Finally, the Maya locals who were serving as our tour guides, in their time crunch to gather all of the food and supplies for an afternoon ceremony, dropped us off with a Maya family who lived on the edge of the market so they could finish shopping without us gawking and slowing them down. The home we visited had three generations living together in a very modest home. Since none of us spoke Spanish (and they didn't speak English), we used Google translator to thank them for welcoming us with their incredible Guatemalan coffee (from my perspective the best in the world). In the awkward silence, Tokala began singing a traditional song. The youngest among them, a baby about 5 months old, cooed and said, "Aho, gracias, wopila" in his own way. We were all thankful for the sacred vibrations that day together. While we couldn't speak the same language, the ancient songs bonded us. About a year later, I was in Guatemala for another gathering, and this same family arrived with the same baby who was now walking. We all embraced like family with the memory of the song medicine that connected us together, that will always connect us in this life and in the next. We make many relatives in life!]

My father died when I was 12 years old. He took a lot of our teachings with him. My own relatives didn't use our Lakota language that much. So, he took a lot of that good energy with him.

When I was 18, I went out to Ohio and stayed for three months in the city. I look at that as a rite of passage for me to go off on my own, to acculturate myself to the White society. I actually met a lot of Black people and started to understand non-Indian culture better. That was when I started to relearn who we are by reflecting myself on other cultures.

Since my dad had passed on, we hadn't practiced our Lakota ways. Then I saw the non-Indian dancing our culture at a pow-wow in Pennsylvania. They call them hobbyists, White people who dress up in Tribal regalia and dance in their own pow-wows. I went to a hobbyist pow-wow in the city. That drum, that sacred vibration, was there at that pow-wow, and I felt it. I started to meet White people who were nice. They welcomed me and got me back to exploring my cultural ways again and helped me to start to learn that not all White people are Long Knives. I wrote a letter to my mom in which I told her that I wanted to dance again and try to go back inside of myself to find out who I am and to help that curiosity grow and be nurtured. I started to remember things, remember what was told to me. I learned to be a fancy dancer.

The early days were good. There was good healthy competition, good sportsmanship.

But when I saw how that competition slowly deteriorated with the introduction of money as prizes, I didn't enjoy myself in that circle anymore. I set it aside in 1976. I tried to go back to the pow-wow **Hocoka**, but the good energy wasn't there anymore. I see that everywhere now. The competition creates people who are trying to run away from themselves rather than trying to enjoy themselves. I tell people if they are going to sing and dance, just enjoy themselves, don't do it for the competition. Just enjoy relatives and sing and dance without alcohol and drugs. Everyone openly shook each other's hands and really did show respect for one another in the old days. Today's pow-wow world really has a lot of pseudo people with fake personalities who are only there for the money. They say things and do things without showing true love, and you can observe that right off the bat. You can feel people's handshake when they really don't mean it. They just do it because it's expected. They really don't care about who you are but are more interested in the competition of winning. When you were asked to judge a pow-wow category, they were only nice to you because they know you are a potential judge. When you are a pow-wow contest judge, they shake your hand and treat you really nice. If you don't pick them during the competition, they are not nice to you anymore. You become a good judge of character if you go down that pow-wow road.

The **Mitakuye Oyasin** (all my relatives) goes beyond the winged ones and the four-leggeds. There are many different levels of **Mitakuye Oyasin**. We don't only have the Animal Nation, we also have the Water, the Rocks, the Trees, and the Air as all of our relatives. Beyond that, the galaxy includes Father, Son, and the Stars as our relatives. **Mitakuye Oyasin** is the spiritual relationship we have with Mother Earth and the galaxy.

I was called to the school one time because a 5th grader was being constantly bombarded by bullying. The bullying was not physical, but emotional. Every day he was bombarded on the school bus, during recess time on the playground, in the hallways—he was constantly made fun of. No one would sit with him at lunchtime. Mentally, he was aware of the teasing and complained to his mom about why he was like he was. This boy had a disability that was the target of the teasing. One evening after school, he decided to take his life. His mom was a hard-working single parent who got off work about ten minutes after the bus dropped him off. When she got home that day and couldn't find her son, she went to the backyard to find him hanging on the clothesline. He had been telling his mother about how all the kids were making fun of him all this time, and then he killed himself.

I was getting gas in that community the same day, and another spiritual leader asked me to help talk to these kids who were traumatized by what happened. I said, "Sure, I'll go help." I asked him to bring the mother to the school, too, because we were going to do some healing to help the mom and the kids. They brought the mom and we met in the school library. The other spiritual leader sat all the kids in a big circle. He brought a drum and sang a prayer song. I talked with the youth and we prayed. They all felt bad for making fun of him and giving him such a bad time. I prayed with the mom and explained to them about how anger can come from both sides. I told them that this mom, she is not going to be with her son anymore, but as a loving mom she has to learn to forgive, and you have to learn how to forgive yourself, too, for all the things you did and said to her son. He was trying to learn to live with his handicap and words hurt. I said, "Today, we are going to do **Wohunka**, a spiritual adoption ceremony. From this day forward, you all are going to be this mom's children. She lost her son, but today she gains all of you as sons and daughters. So when you come up here to hug her or shake her hand, you have to call her Mom." I don't think there was a dry eye in the whole room. I was just passing through that day. I was just getting gas at the gas station when that happened. It wasn't planned.

Hunka (adoption) was brought to us by the White Buffalo Calf Woman when the gift of the pipe was given to us. **Hunka**

is for healing the family through ceremony by replacing relatives who have gone on.

Wocaja
(Receiving a Name)

When we moved to town, it increased my awareness that something was taking care of me. I drowned. We were playing follow-the-leader. In the winter there was a lot of snow, and in the summer a lot of water. That summer, there was a dam that was flooding. Nearby, there were older boys who made a homemade diving board, and they were diving off the board and jumping into the dam. We dared each other to swim across, and the only swimming method we knew was dog paddling. So, there we were, dog paddling across that dam. I was the last one. About half way across, I cramped up and I went down. I remember my feet hitting the muddy bottom and pushing myself up. I did it two or three times and the third time I remember watching the bubbles as I went up and I saw the light above starting to fade away. After that I heard voices. I heard someone say, "Do it again." They were pushing my chest and my chest really hurt. Water came out of my mouth and my nose and they said, "Do it again." And more water came out, and finally I could breathe and I took a hard breath and I started to open my eyes. I was on the beach of the dam, and everyone was standing around looking at me. I kept vomiting and bringing up water and more water. It must have been like a birthing when we took our first breath. Finally, when I was able to talk, I realized that my older cousin, Charlie Long Soldier, had saved me. He was doing the same thing that a midwife did, helping the Spirit into this world, from breathing liquid to breathing air. He saved me from drowning and gave me a chance to breathe air, to live again.

Years later, I went back to Wanbli and honored Charlie by giving him a Star Quilt. I told the people I would not be here today if this cousin had not saved me at Wanbli. I had him tell the story because I was too choked up to tell the story myself. I have a VHS tape of it, and even on the tape you can hear that he got choked up too. It was a really good ceremony.

That was another experience of me staying alive. Going to the Spirit World and coming back again. That's when my family honored me with the Lakota name **Tokala Hocoka Waokiya Ob Mani,** one who spreads blue energy helping the people live. That is my new name. They gave me that name and put a feather on my head. I have been honored three times as **Tokala**. A lot of our people get many names. One of my grandfathers had nine names. My father had five names. When you are born you can carry the name of a grandfather on the paternal side if you are male, or grandmother on the maternal side if you are female. You get those names as a baby to carry that name on. Another way you could get a name is from Spirit or **Tunkasila** that comes from an altar. After that, for every achievement you make, you are gifted with a name. If you are a veteran, you get a name for the sacrifice you make in battle. For every achievement you can get a different name that will be in accordance with that achievement. We had a lot of names. My mom's dad was Carries the Fire, which is a powerful spiritual name. When they put us on the Census, they drew names out of the hat. I think I told you that's how he got the name Silas and they shortened the last name to Fire. My mom's name was Nellie Fire, and her brother was John Fire-Lame Deer (**Tahca Huste** is Lame Deer). He was also a Medicine Man (**Naca**, Chief).

Tiopa Yanni
(Third Door)

Wicasa Winyan Pejuta
(Medicine of Adulthood)

*T*HE THIRD QUARTER is the middle age and is the healing or action stage of the ceremony. Age does not matter, but wisdom counts because some feel younger or older. I believe this is the most important quarter because this quarter is responsible for the first two quarters and the 4th quarter. They're taking care of the first quarter coming into this world, so they are grounded; they are teaching and advising the second quarter; and they also need to help the 4th quarter as they release from this world and go back to the spiritual world. They are also learning from the 4th quarter as they walk by the side of their elders and what is waiting for them, this is after the second rite of passage.

The third quarter carries a lot of weight, because they are responsible for the ones coming in and the ones who are leaving. It's such a vital quarter for life. They need to know the good, the bad, and the ugly. At that age, in the third quarter, you often know the outcomes before they happen. Many times, you can look at a person and know if they are good, bad, or ugly. At that time, you can decide if you want to put your energy into helping that person or not.

During this quarter, the 7th direction becomes very important because you must conserve and preserve yourself to last the long run because you can get tired and sick from too much caring for others. During this quarter, it's like you're standing on the edge of the cliff; if you don't take care of yourself, you'll go over the edge of the cliff. If you go over the edge, we can't pull you back. It's hard to regenerate your energy if you are suffering from cancers and other diseases already. During this quarter, you must really, really, really work on yourself because it is overwhelming. Today when the doctor says a person in the last stage of cancer, people are giving up on them, even doctors are giving up on them. What can we do to help you if you fell off the cliff already?

This is the quarter in which you must start fractionating your energies, good or bad. You must compartmentalize them. You must practice very strong health practices during this time. You can't smoke so much; you must not drink so much. You must know your limitations during this time. For example, you can't stay up all night anymore and hang out with the young ones. If you do, people will say you are foolish, and you become a fool. Instead of respecting you they will laugh at you because you are not taking care of yourself in the stage that you are in. If you don't know your limitations and practice strong self-care during this quarter, you will fall off the cliff.

When a person in the third quarter falls off the cliff, it creates a big impact on the rest of the family in other quarters. Try not to let yourself fall off, but if you do and you are dying early, the rest of the family and friends must surround you and make you feel comfortable. As a human being it is very hard to let go of people you love. It is hard to say goodbye. That's why in our Lakota language we don't have a word for goodbye; instead, we say, "***Toksa ake***." You are going to see them again.

During the third quarter, make plenty of time for the 7th direction so you can fulfill your role in caring for others.

Wowacintanka
(Fortitude, to Believe in Something and Not Give Up)

Power of the People

In 1991, I started a run called Journey to Healing, which was really a Walk-Ride-Run. Our communities ran, walked, and rode horses and bicycles from the 4 directions of a liquor store in Millet County. When it came to our Tribal politicians, it depended on which way the winds were blowing that day as to whether they helped. In a town called Norris, South Dakota, there was a well-known liquor store. It was on the route toward the Black Hills, so if anyone was going to Black Hills, they would go through that town. The liquor store was west of Parmelee. If you stay on that Tribal highway, driving west, you will drive into the North. To the North of Parmelee was the rez until the 1960s, when the Tribal Reservation lands were reduced after the chairman at the time made an agreement with the state. We still have Tribal Districts there called Black Pipe and Corn Creek.

This all started when the students became aware of the amount of alcohol being used on the Reservation, and they asked Sinte Gleska University help address the use of alcohol. Sinte Gleska leadership agreed. In that agreement, they asked the students to do a survey to further validate their proposal to go after grants. The survey went out to all the districts on Rosebud. Two communities, Parmelee and Norris, reported the most alcohol use. Sinte Gleska located a foundation called Robert Wood Johnson, which asked for anyone to submit a proposal of an alternative way of healing from alcohol. When Sinte Gleska submitted a proposal, they used **Lakol Wicoun** (living with Lakota values and ceremony), and it was funded for three years, starting in 1991. I served as the director for the project, and this is how the Walk-Ride-Run came to be.

In working with the community, I was trying to bring the people out of their homes and into the community buildings, where we hosted healing and wellness activities and learning opportunities, but we couldn't get local family members out of their houses. However, in observance with physical activity of sobriety walks, we saw people come out and take part. Each community had an advisory board, and they decided to go with an activity that started at Parmelee and headed to the north liquor store, because we all agreed that the community problems came from the alcohol that was sold at that store. A healing walk was initially talked about, and during those talks, we realized we have a lot of young people who like to run and ride bicycles and horseback. We decided to get as much involvement from the community at all levels, so we expanded the run to include many forms of transportation. We appointed people to coordinate those activities, but during the planning, relatives from the other three directions became interested in what we were doing. We realized that the relatives in all 4 directions were affected by the alcohol from that same liquor store. We decided to go to the other communities to involve them. To the west was Wanbli; north was Corn Creek; east was Swift Bear, Horse Creek, and White River; and south was Parmelee, He Dog, Upper and Lower Cut Meat, and Red Leaf. The run started from each of these communities in the 4 directions and came in toward the center. The center was the liquor store, but we found no support from the north community, so we moved the center of the run to the north. Corn Creek has a pow-wow arena, so we used that as the center of the 4 directions. We went to all the communities to educate them, and we gave them instructions on the healing ceremony of the run.

Prior to the event, we consulted with spiritual Medicine Men and found out that we needed to start from prayer in the 4 directions, stop three times on our way into the Center of the **Hocoka**, and stop in the **Hocoka** (4th stop) to have the Wiping of the Tears conducted by a spiritual person in observance of the community healing. One death in the community impacts everyone in the community, so everyone has been affected by the losses. When we arrived, Calling Back the Spirit and Wiping of Tears were to be conducted at the Center of the **Hocoka**. We were told we had to follow protocol if it was to be successful.

In the first year, each direction selected a coordinator to help the walk/ride/run get started. Participants in each direction were told the event was not a race, but for healing, so everyone had to stick together, stopping 4 times together. Each direction had a staff carrier of the eagle feather, one blessed eagle feather, and no one was allowed to physically pass the staff carrier. Parmelee included the military veterans who led the walkers with the other staffs, too. It was beautiful to see some family staffs come out and help lead the walkers. The veterans stayed in formation—they walked, carrying staffs, all the way from Parmelee to Corn Creek, about 20 miles. Because Parmelee was one of the grant sites, there was an office and a coordinator who carried this energy through the one year of planning and educated the community at all age levels. This energy included weekly Sweat Lodges, weekly meetings in the community building, fundraising, and weekly outreach. At the end of the race, t-shirts were given to the participants—we love our t-shirts in Indian Country! I still have mine. Through all of this work, the liquor store went out of business. It's because we used ceremony that they closed. We prayed it so. The owner of the liquor store had a relative on the County Commission, and there was some illegal business going on there that the federal government found out about and shut them down. What had started in 1991 lasted until 2003 or 2004. Even after the grant ended, the community took control of it, and kept it going for over a decade.

Woapiya
(Healing The Spirit)

Stages of Understanding WoLakota and How Freud Got It Wrong

I liked Sigmund Freud's teaching as it is similar to our teachings, though not completely the same, as Lakota have more understanding of the spiritual. There are three voices in your head. One voice says, "go for it," another voice says, "don't go for it because you'll get in trouble or get hurt," and a third voice says, "don't go for it because it's not right." You can follow any of those voices. Alcoholics can get to a point where they "black out," and yet they get home and they wake up in their bed or on the floor. How do they get home? Lakota believe it is the Grandfather's voice (God) that guides you home when you are in this state. You are moving dirt, so you will follow that voice even though you don't remember doing it.

From the Lakota perspective there is an overpowering voice that comes from the womb and early teachings, from the invisible world. That voice is **Tunkasila**, Grandfather's voice, and it is that voice that brings you home. When I started studying psychology in college, I could relate to this concept of the Id, Ego, and Superego.

However, Freud is very colonial and concrete in his thinking in a way that lacks understanding of the spiritual. When you are blacked out from being drunk, there is no Ego (reality) helping you rationalize, and there is no Superego imposing morals on you from the outside world about what you should do. The only thing to get you home is your Id, your natural instinct that is connected to the Spirit World. Freud refers to the Id as primitive and childish, much like the Europeans referred to Indigenous peoples. The Id is seen as pure instinct, like the devil talking in your ear, while the Superego is seen as morality that is taught to you by the outside world, like an angel talking in your ear. It appears that Freud is teaching us that the Ego should help you overcome your natural instinct (Id) by following the Superego, which is being forced on us by outside moral teachings, which in this country are primarily Christian or Catholic.

So, in the Lakota way, that overpowering voice of the Id is the voice of our Spirit and the one we should be in tune with, not ashamed of. The Superego is, as Freud describes it, the outside world's teaching of morality, and the Ego is what helps us walk the red road of balance between dark and light, good and bad, yin and yang.

The Spirit Path (the path your Spirit takes) is through the Milky Way. As the Spirit is passing through, a grandma like Saint Peter is waiting for you at the junction of the Milky Way to determine if you have fulfilled your Blueprint. If you are not complete, you will come back, be reincarnated to try again. If you are complete, then you go through the Milky Way. Maybe you have been here many life cycles already, then you may die early because you finished your Blueprint, and it was time for you to go through the Milky Way to the Happy Hunting Ground.

That's why I relate Ego as the person's reality, as you are here in the physical world with deeds you need to complete in life. When you give yourself back to Spirit (Id), you shut down and your organs stop. That's how powerful the brain is, because it's listening to the Ego that says, "Hey, we're done, let's go home."

When you are reincarnated, you may come back with scars; physical, emotional, mental, and spiritual scars. How do you learn to let go of those scars every time you come back to this life? If we don't know how to let go, that garbage bag of scars we carry around gets bigger and bigger. If we don't let it go, we bring it back with us into this world and into all the relationships we have in this world. Maybe in one of our lifetimes we kill someone because of that stuff we haven't let go. So, we will always come back as long as we have not completed our Blueprint. We inherit genes, ancestral memory, that comes with us to this earth. When are you finally going to let go? When are you going to empty that garbage bag you've been carrying for all these lifetimes?

For Lakota, the best healing places for letting go are in the Sweat Lodge, Sundance, and Vision Quest/fasting. In the Sweat Lodge you have trapped the physical and mental in there, so you are forced to address what has hurt you at the spiritual core. You're in the dark and back in your mother's womb. You lose your physical presence in there, so those deep wounds can be healed, so you can finally let go. At the Sundance you are mentally, physically, and spiritually practicing the **Wo** by focusing and praying from dawn to dusk. You are praying for something. Then there are breaks when you are waiting for the answer to your prayers. Sundance teaches you your limitations and is a time for the man to equal the woman's cleansing. The releasing of blood and tears helps you let go. When you do a Vision Quest you are placing yourself in a near death experience because you are depriving yourself of food and water. You're consistently saying your prayer over and over and over. When you do that, your **Tiopa** (doorway) to the other world opens and this allows you to release the spiritual, mental, and physical pain you have been carrying. It allows you to cry. The Lakota word for prayer is **Cekiya**, which means, let us cry/pray.

— PART 4 —

Wowakan Glustanpi
(RELEASING/LETTING GO)

Wamayankayo
(LOOK THIS WAY, THIS IS ME)

WHEN I SMELL SAGE, sweetgrass, or cedar I feel very secure because that is what my father did every evening before we went to bed when I was young. He set that foundation. It is the energy of home. The reason why the light bulbs came on when I learned about the imprint stage of infancy is because so many kids are raised to practice our **Wolakota**. I realize when I smell sage or sweetgrass or cedar, my mind and body go back to the early days of being loved as it was imprinted on me. Being nurtured at home and being protected by my family. It's a good feeling! I still carry that today when I smell smudge. A lot of our Sundances have individuals going all over the campground smudging people constantly all day long. I remind our participants where I Sundance that our energies change quickly. If we see someone we do not like, our emotions or energy can change.

For example, a person may see someone they don't like, and they get up and leave the area. I have seen this happen a lot. When a person does that, there is no focus on God. Why are you there if you are still going to have hatred and anger inside of you, and that's going to control you, control your behavior? You have a hard time believing in anything because your anger is controlling you, and that's why you would get up and leave a place of prayer. When a person does that, they are not trying to let it go, it's like they are trying to treasure it. Treasure their anger, their grief.

When you don't heal, it's like pancake trauma, it just layers and gets worse and worse. Think about how we layer pancakes. That's like trauma. It's layers of layers of unresolved trauma. I had to face the people who hurt me or didn't like me, so I could heal. So many of us ran away. We keep running away and never deal with that mental or spiritual scar. Just like physical scars, we can look at it and remember the date, time, and place. We can do the same with mental and spiritual scars. So that smudging is always done to help keep us on task or to keep us positive and in a good place. Smudging is done to help keep us in the right frame of mind, and it's important to teach this to your children.

By the time it came to raise me as the ninth child, my parents were really aware of my presence. They went through trial and error with my siblings in learning how to care for us. That is just one lifetime, but we are told often that the Spirit comes back to earth because it has to come through a full cycle of **Wo**.

I was thinking about the awareness when I knew something was special. Something that I became aware of that I should start to become. I realized I was neglecting something that was taking care of me. There is a word, **Otehika** in our language. That word basically means hard times. I think this is one of the first teachings I came from when I was raised out in the country before we moved into town when I was 9 years old.

After we moved to town, I was in closer proximity to a lot of my older cousins. I would join them when they would play follow-the-leader by the creek. That's when I learned about leadership. I could tell then that some older cousins were nurturing, good leaders because they would give tasks that were not so difficult as they knew we were shorter and not as tall as they were. I also knew those who had negative energy, because they would ask us to do hard things and then they would laugh at us when we failed at the attempt. Follow-the-leader would begin with rock, paper, scissors to find out who would be the leader for that time. When one of us little ones got to be the leader, the older ones would say, "Oh this is going to be easy."

One day, I got a good teaching with my cousins. When playing follow-the-leader, we had to jump across a bridge that spanned the creek. There was a beaver who had cut a tree down that was below the bridge. There was a way to jump from the railing of the bridge to another nearby tree branch. Then my cousins climbed from the tree branch down into the water. One of the negative leaders took us there, and none of the little guys wanted to follow. Some of the older boys said negative things and called us negative names. I didn't want to be called something negative, so I went out beyond my limitations to try to prove something. As the older boys were jumping through this obstacle course off the railing of the bridge, the little ones who didn't want to go just stood there. But I wanted to prove that us little guys could make it, so I got up on the railing and I jumped and fell short of the branch.

I always remember that trauma. It comes back to me in slow motion. It's like in frames. I was falling. All the branches were off of the tree, and it was dying. I was impaled. I have a scar on my left arm. If I had been a few inches to the right, it would have pierced my heart. My skin was tough enough to let me dangle there. All the blood started gushing from my arm. Blood was covering me and all but one of the older boys took off. They saw the blood and how I was impaled, and they left me there. But one of the older boys, Jerry, was a good cousin. He came down and detached me and took me off of the branch. He took his t-shirt off and wrapped it around my arm to stop the blood, and he helped me walk back to my sister's house. He talked to me and nurtured me not to cry.

I knew I was going to get in trouble. One of my sisters was at the house and she almost went into shock when she saw me. She did her best to stop the bleeding and help me fix the wound the best she could. At that time, my mom came back, and my sister told my mom what had happened. My mom asked me first, "Did you learn a lesson?" I told her yes, and then she rushed me to the clinic. She was waiting for a response from me before she helped me. The clinic professionals fixed my arm, but it was a teaching that I've always remembered. It taught me to be careful about which leaders to trust in the future and to know my limitations. It also taught me about the qualities of a good leader, like my cousin who helped me.

All this came back to me later on when I started Sundancing, because it was my first time to release blood from a tree. In my family's Lakota teaching, they talk about how the man releases blood during the 4th day of Sundance to equalize the suffering a woman goes through during her monthly ceremony and 9 months of pregnancy and giving birth. When a young girl is being prepared for womanhood, the women, (aunties, sisters, mothers, and grandmothers) talk to her ahead of time. They prepare this young woman for the first time of her monthly moon ceremony to not be traumatized and to be in harmony and balance with it.

For me to get in balance with that trauma of releasing flesh, I was told I had to experience **Wokakija**, the hard times of our people. At Sundance, we as men release blood to equal our energy with women. The women are taught through their ceremonies that the release of blood makes them sacred. As men, we can't give birth and we can't release that blood each month. Through Sundance once a year, we release blood, which leads us down the path to sacred. We discipline our Spirit for the people. It is one of our strongest men's ceremonies, and it is where a man can cry openly.

In my family, the men give the flesh offering, which releases blood on the 4th day, every 4th year. To heal and cure, we do it through our ceremonies, Sweat Lodge, and our herbs and plants. One of the things I started noticing at our Sundance is that some people are getting carried away with too many piercings and the pouring blood, unnecessarily, for whatever reason. I feel we need to teach our young people those things the proper way, because it's getting out of hand. There is honor and respect for flesh offerings, but some people are doing it for the show. They are not getting the true teachings from God, **Tunkasila**. Some guys want to pierce every hour on the hour.

At another Sundance I observed an individual pierced during a round that wasn't focusing on the tree or his prayer, but on the audience of people coming to take part in the Sundance. When he saw his friend or relative, he would move closer to them and look at them to see their reaction each time he would pull. When he broke skin, the next relative or friend that showed up would tell the intercessors or the leader, "Hook me up, hook me up." It was all for show.

If you have an interpretation of a dream that you need to pierce on any one day or all of those 4 days, then we try to honor your dream. Some dancers who don't have dreams want to pierce every round. When they do that, it loses its meaning and its sacredness.

In our way of life, Spirit World, we not only learn how to survive, but also how we must respect and honor women for what they go through. Teachings must be done for both male and females. The releasing of blood for both males and females is the cleaning of mind, body, and Spirit. Releasing blood is like a prayer. The male and female have the ability to conceive a child, but it is the woman who holds the womb to sustain life. When it is time for her to give life, she needs the other energy of a male, his sperm, to conceive life. If the sperm isn't there, it becomes a prayer because the bleeding will come with her monthly cycle. The womb has all the nutrients it needs for the egg, when it releases it, then it becomes a prayer. A woman would be taught not to get angry if she doesn't get pregnant and instead to pray during her moon time for life to come during another month. Maybe it is **Tunkasila** intervening and there is a reason why. Maybe **Tunkasila** already knows the future and that the woman is not ready to give birth in 9 months.

Today, men don't understand the longest ceremony that women go through: the ceremony of 9 months in bringing a new Spirit into this world and to respect and pray for a healthy baby. What mother eats, baby eats, when mom laughs, baby laughs, when mom cries, baby cries. How you treat your wife or how a female treats herself affects the little one she is carrying. Imagine yourself listening to that heartbeat, that sacred vibration of your mom, for 9 months. Living and breathing the liquid instead of this oxygen or this air.

The **Hocoka** of life, the sacred Circle of Life, is in our blood. It's called a blood cell. The teaching of the blood is important as it connects to our Spirit. I spell blood **We** (pronounced Wey). I remember sitting, listening to grandpas and grandmas, and they could talk all day on that subject, about the blood. After I started to understand DNA and other small cell structures, I realized that our grandparents already knew those things about the blood.

I started to become aware of the gifts I have. Why am I being called upon? I don't go around saying I'm a Medicine Man or wear a big label or tag saying I can help you. During the time when I was trying to find out who I was and trying to learn about my family tree, I began asking questions to my older sisters, brothers, aunties, uncles, mom, and dad. After my dad left this world, I was trying to find the footprints of where I came from. When we were preparing for the Big Foot Ride, I found out that my father's father was a survivor of the Wounded Knee Massacre in December 1890.

My older sister said we were related to the Sitting Bull family, so I got so excited. Woah, maybe I am related to Grandpa Sitting Bull, I thought. There was a vast Ghost Dance in December 1890 at Standing Rock. That is the day Sitting Bull got killed. He was advocating for the Ghost Dance, and the government didn't like that he was ghost dancing. Anyway, I still believe that was a plan to get rid of him, to kill him. When he was killed, the cavalry surrounded the Ghost Dancers. The non-Indian people thought we were trying to have an uprising, but it was the ***Wonihinciya*** (spiritual fear) that we had. Lakota/Dakota/Nakota had a spiritual fear of the encroachment of White people coming daily, taking our land, and the government was not trying to stop them.

Our people began giving up on the pipe religion because the White people kept coming. Some started to believe that and looked for other ways of prayer; they heard of a powerful Medicine Man who had a cure that would stop the White man from coming. That was the Ghost Dance from a Paiute guy named Wovoka. We believe that dreams come to reality. He dreamt that if the people danced in a circular fashion, fasting and praying, all the White people would die or be eliminated, the buffalo would return, all the dead relatives would come back to life. Those three things made the Ghost Dance look attractive for those of us who did not like being a Prisoner of War on the Reservation, under the rule of White people, the "colonizers," through whom we had lost so many of our loved ones. Our Lakota leaders sent Shortbull and Highbear and two others to investigate this man's power from his dream. They went all the way to Nevada to see Wovoka. That's when they saw and learned of the Ghost Dance.

Shortbull and Highbear and the two others brought that Ghost Dance back to the people. During the last Ghost Dance at Standing Rock, there was talk that they would be killed, massacred right there. They sent all the children and a few warriors with the grandmas to talk to Chief Bigfoot, aka Spotted Elk. They heard that Bigfoot was a good speaker and thought he could advocate for and protect us. All we were trying to do was pray and dance. They snuck off, 300-plus women, grandmas, children, and a few warriors. But when they got to Bigfoot, he was sick. He said I can't help you now, but the group should go to Red Cloud. The U.S. President had listened to Red Cloud before and respected Red Cloud's voice.

Meanwhile, a notice went out by telegram to the cavalry that there was about to be an uprising again. The cavalry came by train from Omaha or Sioux City, down that way, and intersected our group on their way to Red Cloud and took them to Wounded Knee. They took any weapons they might have had, and then they massacred them. The cavalry was the worst one they sent. It was the 7th Cavalry. It was the same one that wanted revenge from the Battle of the Little Big Horn when Custer had been killed. That was the 7th Cavalry. They wanted revenge.

Archeologists uncovered a lot of whiskey bottles at the site of Wounded Knee. Maybe they had to get themselves all liquored up so they could butcher us the next day. Even American Horse witnessed 4 boys who came out of the bush. They didn't want to come out of the bush, but the cavalry coaxed them out, claiming they would take the boys to Red Cloud, and then they hacked them to death. They butchered them and my grandpa survived all that.

Earth Nation Woman, my great-grandma, saved my grandpa that day. She put blood on their faces and covered the blanket in blood, and when the cavalrymen came up on them, they were covered with the blanket and did not move. If anyone moved, the cavalry would kill us to make sure we were dead. They came up the creek looking for survivors. That was the first trauma; maybe there were more traumas that my grandfather survived.

Robert Two Elk was my grandpa's name. He's the one who survived with his sister. My great-grandmother Earth Nation Woman fled to the Stronghold with five grandchildren after escaping Wounded Knee. No cavalry came to the Stronghold, so they moved from the Stronghold to Wanbli to live with the Standing Bear family before the children were sent off to boarding schools. A lot of the young people who survived the massacre were called **Wablenica**. It means homeless or parentless children. A lot of our young children, due to massacres and viruses that came later and killed adults, were left homeless.

Tiopa Topa
(THE 4TH DOOR)

Wakan Elderhood

THE 4TH QUARTER is being an elder and it is the 4th stage of ceremony, which is releasing, when a person has one foot in the door of the invisible (spiritual) world. Today, senior citizens are recognized around age 55–60 and older. However, there is not really a set age, as it is when you go through elder menopause. In this quarter you are recognized and respected for your wisdom. When a person is glowing, that is the energy of *Wo*; they grew up learning the *Wo* and it is within them. When you glow, doors open for you because people can see or observe that you have the *Wo* and will go above and beyond to help you or make you feel better. Those elders who are not brought up in the *Wo*, they may be demanding, greedy, blaming, or selfish. They don't understand the *Wo*. When you can see that an elder does not have the *Wo*, you will avoid them, so you don't get hurt by them. These elders are also not missed when they are gone. In fact, relatives may be happier when they are gone rather than when they are alive, if they don't carry the *Wo*. For those who have the *Wo*, they are loved so much they are memorialized after they pass because they left such sacredness behind.

An elder is a walking, living library with the potential to teach much to the quarters coming up behind them. They are gatekeepers. At that age, they know who to open their gates to and share their energy with. Elders will not waste time on those who are not receptive, as they don't have much time left. Elders usually find a young person in their family or community who they may really mentor to pass along all that knowledge. They look for a person they may unload all their knowledge on, one who has the fortitude and other good values to carry it on.

My dad was an example of this. In the 12 years I knew him, he tried to do his best to teach me. Sometimes I felt really overwhelmed about some of the things he was sharing with me. He prepared me to live and get along with boys older than me. I felt more comfortable with the older boys than I did with my own age group because of my dad's older years and what he taught me to retain; he made me older in my mind and Spirit. I never refused him when he exposed me to my grandpa and uncles' altars, and I wanted to know more. Spirits that come and go, make themselves visible and invisible. Hearing voices, seeing things, things that you share and don't share from that invisible world. It helps me understand that when elders are ready to leave this world, they will say they see a relative who is waiting for them nearby. They feel more relaxed and are not so scared to go. This 4th quarter is about the end of life. It is about leaving the knowledge, the sacredness, and the gifts so that we may pass on to the Spirit World.

I told you how a year after my father passed on, my mom put me in a boarding school. I was 13; I heard of an Indian educator who had gone to the same boarding school for Episcopalians that I went to. He had a reputation at the school of being an athlete, a college graduate, and he was doing good. I finally met him in my debut in the pow-wow circuit as a Fancy Dancer. He was a traditional dancer. I immediately wanted to be like him. He was my first positive role model. This man is Dr. A. C. Ross (Alan

Chaske). I was **Hunka** (adopted) into his family as a brother after we got to know each other better.

Chaske spoke of the Red Road, in living a life of balance and harmony, and then things started to click in my head, and I said *ahhhhh ha!* again. My mom's name is **Canku Luta Win** (Red Road Woman), and I remembered her talking about the Red Road, being in balance and harmony.

Before European exposure, the women had even more ceremonies than men. Because of that, they were more **Wakan** or sacred because they are co-creators of life. They are co-creators with God. Women were mindful of it, so they watched what they said, what they did in their physical, mental, and spiritual ways. They watched how they took care of themselves, so they would not upset that balance within them. When a woman reaches menopause, it is an awareness that during the first puberty rite, everything a woman needs to know physically, mentally, and spiritually is taught by the grandmas (the **Wo, Wa, Wi, We**). How to be a woman, wife, mother, and grandmother. After menopause, the second rite of passage, elders were considered **Tanka** (wise, more galactic with our wisdom). Once a woman has gone through the second rite of passage, she has reached the stage where she can now be involved more with ceremony. As a woman, she no longer has a menstrual cycle, so she can be around ceremony and ceremonial objects without disrupting that from the power that occurs from a menstrual flow. It gives a woman a more powerful voice and she has more balance in life after menopause. Spiritually, she has more respect within the **Hocoka** and is being asked to do more teaching. The 4th quarter of life is the Wisdom Keepers and at the same time she is preparing herself for the exit of this life and the entrance to the next world.

When a man reaches the state of menopause, the men are usually married, and the wife knows when it happens to him. There is a mutual respect of one another between male and female partners and an understanding of the last quarter of life. Once an elder accepts the 4th quarter that their time is limited here, they will work to do what needs to be done to complete their Circle of Life. Many different cultures promote staying as young as possible. In our Lakota way, we accepted our age and energies with our family and acknowledged the time we had left in this last quarter, what needs to be completed, and helping our family complete it. Younger generations should know about the 4th quarter, as it is unavoidable. They should go into the 4th quarter with ease and feeling in harmony with it.

My best advice is to think of oneself as a prayer as you go through during the 4 quarters of life. In the beginning, you were a prayer. If you reach that certain age of the 4th quarter, they will say at this time you are considered a respected elder. You can't go back to being a young person again. You also can't hang around with young people because you are at a different level and you will get hurt. You are not a spring chicken. Youth have energy that can hurt you. Each quarter of life, you have new limitations.

Families who practice the old way have a more peaceful 4th quarter because they have good teachings and energy about it. My mother-in-law, when she was given a terminal diagnosis, just accepted it. She did not run all over the country trying to extend her life. On the other hand, don't give up right away. Don't throw in the towel too soon when it's your time to pass over. When you give up, you let your body quit functioning, so you die quicker. Keep that fortitude throughout your life so you can live as long as you are supposed to. When doctors give a terminal diagnosis, that's "throwing in the towel" advice. Be careful not to give up on your life too quickly, and be wary of doctors who try to predict when you will die.

Today, some would try to bend that universal law to extend their life, and that's when the pharmaceutical prescriptions follow. In the old days, a person would have to complete certain protocols interpreted for them from the Medicine Man for them to get healthy. If the protocols were not completed as specified, then things would happen that could be harmful. If the protocol from the Medicine Man isn't followed, the healing will not be complete. A person may almost be done with their Blueprint, but they still have one last trauma, tragedy, or suffering that they have to experience. No one can stop it because it is a part of their Blueprint. It's heartbreaking when a child dies or when someone is killed before their time. Those are major traumas that take time to heal. That child or person is in a better place in the Spirit World, and you will see them again after you go. But it's up to you to make it there. Oftentimes, when someone passes, you can feel the energy coming back in a new baby. When you get that feeling that the new baby reminds you of the energy of someone who has gone, that may be them coming back to try to finish their Blueprint.

That's why there is never a goodbye. It's only until we see each other again.

When you go into the 4th quarter with proper teachings, your life energy is to be a leader to your family. I know elders who are dealing with a lot of pain, but they don't tell anyone how much pain they're going through. I really respect that. They are not complaining about death but focusing on living the physical life they have left. It helps the younger people develop good resiliency in moving into the 4th quarter of life.

I feel that it is time for myself to start speaking up (bravery) for what I said I would do for the youth and families in my last quarter of life. If I do not say these things, this generational trauma is going to continue. We need to take action as soon as possible. We need to start developing a unity of concerned people to start gathering to make this change. To go beyond the family circles and look at the bigger picture to address the lawmakers, and to educate them about universal law, before it's too late. One voice is like a puppy barking in the wind. We need to start to gather all voices of our concerned relatives on Turtle Island to address this threat to our existence, and we need to join our voices on a global scale across Mother Earth.

In our journey of survival, we need to share leadership with one another. We don't have time for Lone Rangers. The time is now! We have no time to lose. We have a tsunami of ***Wicokuja*** that is coming. It is here already. If we do not unite for healing, our ***Hunupa*** (two-leggeds) might not be around much longer. While the rich are busy trying to develop a spaceship to take their energy of greed to another planet, we, the common people, need to find ways of survival.

We have no other choice but to use the power of prayer and the power of love. That is where the universal law comes from.

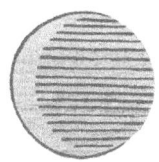

Woasnikiya
(Giving Your Spirit, Mind, and Body Rest and Relaxation)

*B*EAR BUTTE IS A GATHERING PLACE for the people to come and live together for a period of time. I feel this because it's a graveyard for our people. It is a place where the 4th part, the releasing, of the ceremony occurs. It's the end of your grieving period. One of our sacred rites is keeping of the soul or keeping of the Spirit (***Nagi***). There is a releasing because after a person dies, they would place the body of their relative on a sacred hill on a scaffold. This was done to give back to (feed) the winged-nation first. We gave our flesh and blood back to those we took from. This went on for one year. Then the bones were taken down from the scaffold and buried.

When Crazy Horse was killed at Fort Robinson, his grandpa and grandma came after his body in a wagon and took him to a hill in Nebraska. I was told that on the west side of that hill, there is a high place where they placed his body on a scaffold for one year.

In pre-colonial days, the Seven (7) Council Fires identified a plateau in the Black Hills as one of our burial places that people used, depending on their location. All of the Council Fires brought their bones to be buried there. It was a place of releasing, and the time to end the grieving after one year of feeding the birds. Many people traveled by foot before the horse came to our people, and after. How long it took for them to complete the journey would depend upon many factors, such as weather as well as the wishes of the person who had died, who ultimately determined where their bones would be buried. Once the people arrived, the spiritual leader for the family would support the ceremony process. Sometimes, the spiritual leader was selected from another **Oceti** Council Fire, and the family may have to camp out to wait for them to arrive. They may be at the burial site for one or two weeks, and the ceremony would occur during that time.

One of our sacred numbers is 4. There were at least 4 days of ceremony for releasing. During that time, the spiritual leaders told the families to cry and do other things they needed to do to release their pain, following proper protocol. In the old days, the women in some families practiced the releasing of blood as an act of grieving, by cutting the wrists, because they missed their loved one. In the film *Dances with Wolves*, Kevin Costner came upon a grieving bleeding White woman, a widow who was married to a Lakota warrior. Costner chased her, thinking he was saving her because she was bleeding. All the while, she was running away from him because she wanted to complete her ceremony (**Wasigla**). Then the people of the camp got mad at Kevin Costner's character, Lieutenant Dunbar, for bringing her back. A person will come back when they are done grieving, whatever time that takes. In our Lakota way, after European religions arrived, if a person wants to show their love for their spouse who has passed on, they will wear black. If a person wants to remain grieving, the community will let them.

How long a ceremony lasts will depend on when everyone in the ceremony believes that they have done all they need to do to release. Time is not experienced according to a clock, but rather, a feeling that it is done. This is good because then they can go home happy. The releasing takes a heavy load off their back.

The Black Hills is a Grieving Summit, I call it.

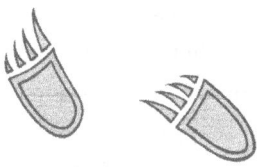

Iya
(Releasing the Monster)

Unci Maka (Grandma Earth Spirit) comes to our communities as the image of a grandma and visits you while you sleep. She visits all the 7 Council Fires in our subconscious and asks the question, "Who are you?" As a living miracle of dirt, we can change.

When I graduated with my undergraduate degree and worked as a teacher, I started teaching our youth and observing inappropriate behavior in the classroom. This inspired me to go back to school to get a graduate degree to dig deeper to find a reason why our children have that violent and disrespectful behavior. From that time on, I feel like I've been on a safari in a jungle of alcohol and drugs, trying to find the why, and a cure for it. Behind me on my safari, I have teachers, principals, police, priests, medicine people, and social workers who all want to know why our children are so inappropriate. Today, we know where it's coming from. It's coming from our homes. What I have learned on my safari is that, inside that same dwelling that used to be **Wakan** (sacred), now live Monsters, whether they are conscious of that yet or not.

So much so, that our own youth are trying to run away by taking their own lives, or by turning to alcohol or drugs.

I worked eleven years with our Tribal children's court, and I found more youth who have been traumatized many times in their upbringing within their own homes. For me to learn why there is so much inappropriate behavior in our classrooms is for me to learn that all this inappropriate behavior is coming from the home, and it spills out to the rest of the world.

From my own personal experience, I was a youth who had a good, loving mom and a good, loving father up to the age of 9. I had a family from a good home who supported me to succeed. However, even if we grow up in a loving home, once we leave that home, we are exposed to that inappropriate behavior that is spilling out of other homes. You can be the best mom and best dad in the world, but once your kids are exposed in the classroom or hallway to bad energy, or Monster behavior, they are exposed to **Wicokuja**. That Monster is in the parking lots, it's on the playgrounds, it's on the school buses, and it's in the community. Our adults are not aware, are so assimilated, or are so used to this Monster, it has become the norm. They have a tolerance for the Monster and the crisis that is created. Monster behavior has become acceptable.

One Christmas when I was working for a Tribal boarding school, there were nine youth that begged us to keep the dorms open for Christmas. They didn't want to go home. They would say, "Mr. Two Elk, our homes are not like that. They are not good places. Can you keep the dorms open for us?" It really made me sad. Young people who didn't want to go home.

There used to be loving grandpas and grandmas who had that **Wo** teaching, that **Wo** love. They are almost all gone, so there is a missing link.

When a baby comes into a Monster home, they are imprinted to becoming a Monster, so the schools have a hard time teaching them discipline because there is no concept of good or morality for that child. Our children are in school for 6–8 hours a day, 5 days a week, for 9 months. This provides a prime opportunity to help fill that missing link. We could start as early as Head Start, sharing stories about good and bad behavior, teaching universal laws.

That's what grandma and grandpa used to do. They would teach you those things. They did this without spanking or other violent behavior.

Without these grandparent teachings, at least for children who are living in Monster homes, the only place they might receive those teachings is at school. Schools can also be an educator for parents in Monster homes to learn about the *Wo*. The courts can also serve this role. One time I was working in the Juvenile Detention Center with a Tribal clinical psychologist who said, "It's sad that today we have to have the court order our parents to love their children."

I can always tell when someone has been taught traditionally. I can see how they exhibit good manners as compared to those who were not taught traditionally.

It's sad to me how a lot of our youth are exposed to alcohol and drugs in the womb. They can't help it when they come into this world already with handicaps or inappropriate behavior. A lot of the psychiatrists prescribe drugs to these youth because it's a damage that is really hard to change. When the damage to a child occurs in the womb, sometimes medication may be the only thing that works. For some of these youth, medication may be the only way that some of them are going to make it in this world.

For youth who are damaged outside of the womb after birth, through exposure to trauma, they can be fixed. Unfortunately, many of these youth are prescribed drugs that don't allow for real healing to occur, which creates another addiction for them to overcome. I started working at our Juvenile Detention Center and I learned that about 95 percent of our youth were on a mental health drug to deal with diagnosed ADHD or other problematic behaviors that originate from trauma. Working in this job also taught me a lot about parenting, and the impact of historical trauma that leads into intergenerational trauma that all resulted from boarding schools and other historical and spiritual wounds. I learned that the behavior that we carry gets passed down, from generation to generation.

One of the questions that always comes up when working with helpers, whether they are Tribal or non-Tribal professional people, is, "What is the Cure?" or "Where is the Cure?" It's hard to help our people do things in a good way, to help them heal, without them getting angry with you. They get angry because they have been living like this for generations now, and they are so used to the chaos that it has become acceptable; the Monster, it's become their way of survival. They are in survival mode. Monster parenting, I call it. Teaching children how to do more damage than you did.

I learned that we, as two-leggeds, come from the animal world, and we have learned survival techniques and have gotten used to them. The world of psychology calls these survival techniques "fight or flight," as I referenced earlier. That can be healthy when there is a real threat, and it saved our ancestors lives during times of attempted genocide, which is why we are still here today. However, a lot of times that "fight or flight" can be very unhealthy, especially when there is no real threat present. I've seen a lot of young people survive in the rez jungle and in the urban jungle: those nightmarish jungles of drugs and alcohol in their families, community, apartments, and homes, and how the youth develop a resiliency to survive. They don't think about what they are doing. They don't think at all. To them, it's just surviving. Even if it is criminal behavior that's helping them survive.

An example would be stealing from a home for whatever you need, food or other goods that you can resell to get what you need. Another example would be joining up with a gang and seeing the gang as more of a family than your own family. For many young people, the gang helps them more than their own family does, even if the gang help is unhealthy. They find safety and security that they don't have in the home. They will even endure the pain of gang initiation to have the safety and security that's missing. Then they grow to respect that behavior, even though it is unhealthy. They grow up with that violent gang mentality, they respect it and even brag about it. Young girls are being called that "b" word and being treated like that and living with the gang code to survive. A lot of the communities have active gangs who now cause more problems for our families. Throw on a big dose of drugs, the selling of drugs or alcohol, or worse, human trafficking, and that creates another avenue for our youth to go in that direction. Some go by choice and others by force.

For as far back as I can remember, those of us who grew up on the Reservation, grew up in depression. Some people left this depression and moved to the cities. Some have learned to respect our **Wo** ways by being raised traditionally and to respect our way of life. I never thought we were poor when I was a kid, because my dad always put food on the table and my mom always cooked. I never saw violence in our home. In the country, I never saw my dad hit my mom or my mom hit my dad. In the country, we had a very loving home. But when we moved to town, I saw my dad become an alcoholic and abuse my mom. I was 9 years old the first time I saw this abuse at home. It created a lot of anger for me. Later in life, I did not realize that my sole purpose for using alcohol and drugs myself was because of my unresolved anger, the pancaking traumas I never resolved. It drove me to extended days of binge-drinking alcohol so that I did not have to deal with reality.

Until one day I woke up on September 12, 1985, and the only way I could put a stop to my abuse of my body, my mind, and my Spirit was to start working on myself, to start working toward my Blueprint to become a more productive human being. That meant letting go of my anger. That meant forgiving other people, including myself, my father, and my past relationships. That meant, letting go of some of my childhood traumas. I call it "spiritual reawakening." I had to make my commitment at a sacred place, and I chose Bear Butte to make that connection. I have a lot of respect for Bear Butte. I hear so many stories of our past leaders receiving their visions there. That is a place where there is a doorway for talking to **Tunkasila** (God), and it helped when I went there. I still remember the day. From that time on, every June, I go to Bear Butte and make my prayers, in the spring when the Thunder People come back. We used to go to Bear Butte to pray in April, but now, because of climate change, there is pollution and other environmental shifts that have snow on the mountain later than usual, so we go in June.

I do not go to be a Medicine Man, but to say thanksgiving for the past year, for **Tunkasila**'s (God's or Grandfather's) help and to make prayers for the future for the coming year, for whatever road that Grandfather has prepared me to take. Since 1985, I feel this calling to do things that bring me knowledge, and I have to use all my values of bravery, generosity, fortitude, and wisdom because it's so easy to give up on helping our people.

So many people are not ready to change their behavior. I remember my grandfather saying, "When you choose this way of walking, this way of prayer with our sacred **Canupa**, our sacred pipe, some people are not going to like you. They may throw rocks at you, call you names, and even spit on you." He didn't really mean to spit on you, he was just saying that to make a point that you would experience negativity from others who were not healthy or ready for change.

But you must find that balance for yourself, despite how others will treat you. It was hard in the 1990s to come back and raise my children. In 1992, my daughter came, and I gave her my great-grandma's name Earth Nation Woman after my great-grandmother who helped my great-grandfather survive Wounded Knee. My son came in 1994, and I gave him my great-grandfather's name, Walks with Two Elk Medicine. Walks is another form of saying Lives, so my son's name is also Lives with Two Elk Medicine.

I look at my two children as two pills that my grandfather gave me to help me live after almost killing myself with alcohol. They gave me a reason to live. I'm glad that my children were not exposed to the alcohol that I was exposed to. That's what I want them to know, an alcohol- and drug-free life, or the ***Wo*** life. It was a big decision to catch the fragments of that fractionated energy of what's left of the ***Wo*** (Sacred Energy) of our people. Catching the fragments and putting them back together again as a whole. People still exist who have the ***Wo***, but, because it went underground, it's hard to find. The priest used to peek into people's windows to see if they were using the pipe. Because of the fear of persecution from European religions and colonizers that was forced upon us, those who know ***Wo*** will only open their door, ***Tiopa***, if they trust you, so it's hard to find the real ***Wo***.

As I shared, there are many false, self-made spiritual leaders who create confusion and false hope for those in search of finding ***Wo***. The ones who ask for money up front or say they expect something from you, are the self-made ones who are trying to make a name for themselves in a selfish way. On my search for ***Wo***, I found out that there were very few relatives who have that ***Wo*** energy left. There are many relatives who carry jealousy, anger, and other unhealthy or negative behavior that I don't want my kids exposed to. We have so many lost people out there wandering aimlessly around without humility.

One of the ingredients for ***Wo*** understanding is that a person needs to understand our Lakota language to best understand the ***Wo***. As reported by the Rosebud Language Preservation Office, in 2014 there were 2,000 fluent Lakota speakers on the Reservation. By 2018, there were about 400. In less than 4 years, it dropped that fast. It makes some people worry about the future, but some don't care anymore, or maybe they have learned helplessness and respond with apathy.

When I was growing up, I watched and heard those who were disobedient, living inappropriate lifestyles, and the elders would say, "Let them go. Whatever they are looking for, they will find it." That was what a grandma who came into the wake service said as she pointed to her grandson's casket. She said, "I'm not going to cry. I already cried enough, and he did not listen. I hope he is happy, wherever he is, and found whatever he was looking for."

That was very humbling for a grandma. There was nothing left for her to do but to let go of the memory she had of her grandson.

It's hard to be humble today because the true teaching of ***Wo*** comes through the language. ***Wo*** teaches us humility in the spiritual context. Without the language you lose the potency of ***Wo***, and you don't get the true understanding of humility.

The European's written history, called the Bible, says the meek shall inherit the earth one day. Humility is very important in finding ***Wo*** across spiritual beliefs. If you don't have it, someday you are going to experience it. Some who have never understood humility may even commit suicide. A well-known champion traditional dancer went to court on multiple occasions, and the judge said he would serve six months in jail. When the police were on the way, he hung himself instead of facing six months in jail, the consequences of not knowing humility. It is a learning process to be humble. We've been through humility, our Native people. We experienced starvation, drought, viruses, and murder, and we came through all of it. Those are major teachings of humility.

The good news is that a lot of us have the DNA of the Wolakota inside of us, even those who don't know the language yet. You can feel it, even if you can't speak the language, you can feel it. I think that goes across the board with all of our Tribes.

To begin to pull together the fractions of ***Wo***, I searched within myself because I grew up with altars and had relatives in my life who I was exposed to and who could open the doorway, ***Tiopa***. They would always say to me, "Wherever you go on Mother Earth, we can find you." It's kind of like the mafia, but in a good way. Buffalo Horn Chips, Moves Camp, Carries the Fire, Arrow Side, Kills Enemy, Runs Above, Poor Thunder, Fools Crow, Two Dogs, and Carries His Sacred Pipe supported me in my journey to finding the real ***Wo***.

Once you start to find yourself and work on yourself and let go of some of these bad teachings and replace them with good teachings, then you are on your way to holistic healing. I feel that a lot of young people go so far, and then they quit. There are many unhealthy teachers out there. After I started to understand the practice of **Wo**, I began to encounter grandmas and grandpas who changed their behavior in a negative way because of boarding school. I follow my parents' teachings and tell my relatives not to spend time with those who have that unhealthy behavior in their search for **Wo**.

Bringing our children back and trying to raise them in our homelands, well, what we have left of our homelands, is going to be important to catch that **Wo** energy again. That is just some of my personal sharing of my life—to help other relatives become stronger and healthier, because it's good when people work together and help those who need help.

I remember one time I was sitting thinking about what else is needed to put in this book, and I wanted to include some of the **Wo** words, some of the **Wa** words, some of the **Wi** words, and some of the **We(h)** words. Grandmas and grandpas can talk about those words all day long. I've heard them talk about blood **We(h)** for a long time—the awareness that the world's smallest **Hocoka** (Circle of Life) is in our blood. It's so small you must use a microscope to see inside that blood cell. Inside that blood cell is the Circle of Life. There is a nucleus and inside that nucleus are all the grandpas and all the grandmas on your dad's side and your mom's side. The blood cell carries oxygen to the brain, and then it dies and is released. That ceremony of calling, welcoming, healing, and releasing is all within the blood because the blood cell only stays alive for so long. Before microscopes came to our people, our grandmas and grandpas already knew these things. They already knew the world was round.

They knew that invisible world of creation, love. That's the main ingredient for life. They knew how we came to this world and how we sustain energy in this world. We, the Lakota, were aware of that transfer from the physical to the spiritual, which revolutionized the Wolakota way of life. We are the ones who know the connection to our galactic relatives. And that is superior! When you compare the Lakota to the Greedy Ones who killed and hurt others in the claim of superiority, it is clear there is no comparison. If you are superior, you have respect for life. You can be the first to be a leader in your family who makes the change from an unhealthy to a healthy home by educating yourself and seeking out examples of healthy people who are living that way of life. You don't have to be perfect at it, you just need to be the first and to give good effort every day.

The grandmas and grandpas knew about balance because they knew the teaching of ***Wo***, and they sacrificed everything not to lose it. I feel that what the grandpas and grandmas fought and died for was that teaching of ***Wo***. It was something good. Beyond good, it was sacred, and they wanted to hang on to that teaching and pass it down to the future generations.

So, it begins. . . .

There is hope. You are the hope. ***Mitakuye Oyasin*** (all my relatives).

— THE HEALING —

Ina Maka Wiconi

Chante Waste Ya Canku Luta / Akan Mauani

Wopila—Pilamiya yelo
Spirit Thanksgiving

During our walk here on **Ina Maka,** (Mother Earth) always give thanks for the blessings, the gifts that **Tunkasila** gives you, such as your children, and their health, your vision/sight, your ears, your ability to walk. Do not take these gifts for granted.

Have a happy journey here on Mother Earth *(Ina Maka).*

Tokala Hocokan Waokiya Ob Mani He Miye Yelo.

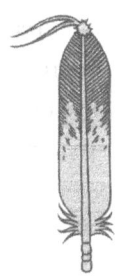

Appendix

Wowahokunkiya *(Spiritual Advice for Survival)*	Description
Wo *(Spiritual Energy)*	Energy of the cosmos, there is an invisible energy we must live in balance with.
Living Energy	Energy of all things that live, all things have opposite, good/bad, life/death, 4 quarters in the Circle of Life.
Mother Earth	From her comes the life force of living energy, she gives us everything we need to live, and we respect and honor her for it. We give back to her.
Blood	Blood is the footprint of creation that comes into the physical world and then returns to the invisible world, and our blood must mix (be diverse) to survive.
Bravery	Standing strong with courage and facing fear helps you grow.

Fortitude	Standing strong in your beliefs, when you have doubt it creates weakness, you must believe to overcome adversity. Fortitude takes the practice of patience and the ability to endure pain and sacrifice.
Humility	We are a common energy that has life, we accept ourselves without power (or perfection) because we understand power greater than us.
Wisdom	To be in balance and harmony with the past, present, and future.
Generosity	The power to help live. Caring for others. Sharing what you have in generosity with others.
Numbers	Everything comes in fours, the Tatuwe Topa (sacred 4) directions, the cycles of life, the cycles of ceremony, the seasons. The numbers 7, 12, and 28 are also significant. Seven is Sakowin, and this includes the direction of what is in the sky, what is under the earth, and yourself. Twelve is the number of rocks for Inipi (Sweat). Twenty-eight is the number of male/female pairs supporting the traditional government of the Oceti Sakowin Oyate, 4 pairs from each of 7 Council Fires.

7th Direction	You are the 7th direction. Where you are you orient to the other 6 directions. The 7th direction is the most important for your survival. You must work on yourself, the 7th generation, so that where you are is sacred and what you bring is sacred.
Courtship/ Approval/Marriage	Union to bring new life is a bond made forever.
Blueprint	Cycle from the Spirit to the physical, always evolving for completion of your life course. Disruption in the Blueprint will result in reincarnation. Once the Blueprint is completed you can pass to the Happy Hunting Ground beyond the Milky Way.
Trauma	Woakipa (trauma) Wo is both negative and positive, as is trauma. Like a woman giving birth or a man piercing in Sundance, this is a good trauma. Violence or serious accidents are bad traumas. You must learn how to receive and balance the trauma you receive in life. When a person experiences Kante (kills the nerve to live), you must have ceremony to heal yourself.
Life and Death	Life is calling, welcoming, healing, and releasing to death. You must respect life, and you cannot extend life beyond the time for that life to exist.

Taking Life	You must defend your blood, and in the process of defending you may take life. When you take life you must participate in a healing ceremony and the power of the drum to regain your heart balance.
Adoption	For the losses in the family circle, there is a protocol for replacing that relative through adoption, used for healing a wound.
Having Pity and Compassion	You must have compassion on others because you are also pitiful.
Calling for Death	You must not do things that call for death or it will come. Do not allow children to pretend about death, do not wish to die, do not wish others to die.
Prophesy	Innocent ones of the Animal Nation can bring messages of the future, spiritual appearances and interventions occur in life.
Keeping Your Word	There is an energy of trust, in the energy of who we are, we must honor our word.
Karma	What energy you put out will always come back to you.

Tokala Two Elk
His Life in Photos

Tokala as a boy

Claude Morris Two Elk, graduation yearbook, 1972

Tokala in college, 1974

Tokala's son, Hehaka, 2012

Tokala's son, Hehaka, and daughter, Tuki, at graduation, 2012

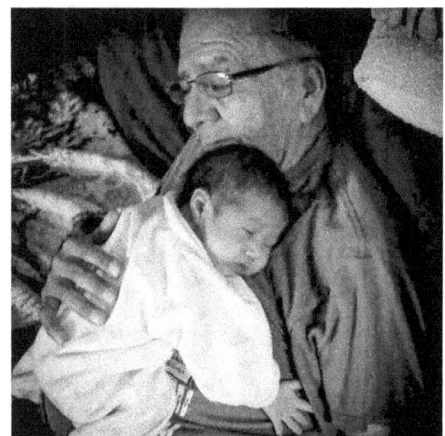

Tokala and his grandchild Xavier, 2013

Tokala and his children, Hehaka, Nellie (Tuki), and first grandchild, Xavier, 2014

Tokala and his son, Hehaka, at Sheridan Lake, Hesapa, Black Hills, 2014

Tokala at Cannonball, Standing Rock, Water Protectors, Mni Wiconi, 2015

Tokala and John Beheler at the Lower Brule
Circle of Care trailer, 2016

Tokala at Glacier Park, near Browning, Montana, 2018

Tokala with Pedro Chan, Maria Camey Huz, and Alfonzo Rafael at the Sicangu Rosebud Lodge, June 2018

Tokala and his daughter, Tuki, 2019

Tokala and his grandchild Eli, 2019

Tokala and J. D. Jones, Guatemala, 2019

Tokala and J. J. Lind, Around the Fire, Guatemala, 2019

Tokala and J. J. Lind, Guatemala, 2019

Tokala in San Pedro, Lake Atitlan, Guatemala, 2019

Tokala with Maya relatives

Tokala's two grandchildren, Xavier and Eli, 2019

Tokala in Chimaltenango, Guatemala, March 2019

Tokala in the market in Chimaltenango, Guatemala, March 2019, with Alfonzo Rafael, J. D. Jones, and Pedro Chan

Colombia – February 2020 at the Indigenous organization of Antioquia

Tokala getting a ride down the mountain in Colombia by the park rangers, February 2020

Tokala speaking to College Students of the Pedagogy of Mother Earth Program at the University of Antioquia, Medellín, Colombia, February 2020

Tokala with Pablo Tisoy and J. D. Jones in Medellín, Colombia, February 2020

Tokala and his grandchildren, 2021

Tokala *(2nd from the right)* and Naca (Lakota Leaders) at the Oceti Sakowin Treaty Meeting, December 2021

Tokala being filmed for a documentary in White Oak, Cherokee Nation, May 2021

Tokala being filmed at Osage Nation
by J. J. Lind and Brooke Allen, 2022

Tokala and his son, Claude Miles Two Elk, 2023

Tokala and his family at his daughter's graduation
with a master's degree, 2023

Osage Nation, April 2023, Tokala with
Alfonzo Rafael, J. D. Jones, and J. J. Lind

Three generations—Tokala, Hehake, and Eli

Tokala and his grandchild Xavier, unknown year

www.ingramcontent.com/pod-product-compliance
Lightning Source LLC
Chambersburg PA
CBHW072042160426
43197CB00014B/2590